FOR REMEMBRANCE
SOLDIER POETS WHO HAVE FALLEN
IN THE WAR

Photo by *Sherril Schell*.

RUPERT BROOKE,
SUB-LIEUT. R.N.V.R.

FOR REMEMBRANCE

SOLDIER POETS WHO HAVE FALLEN IN THE WAR

BY

A. St. JOHN ADCOCK

'If his dust is one day lying in an unfamiliar land
    (England, he went for you),
O England, sometimes think of him, of thousands only one,
In the dawning, or the noonday, or the setting of the sun,
    As once he thought of you.'
        LIEUT. H. REGINALD FRESTON.—*The Gift*.

HODDER AND STOUGHTON
LONDON   NEW YORK   TORONTO
MCMXVIII

Note

THE Author's thanks are due to the relatives, friends and publishers of the Soldier Poets referred to in this volume for kindly lending him portraits, supplying biographical information, and giving permission for the use of extracts; to Viscount Wolmer for a copy of the lines by his brother, Captain the Hon. Robert Palmer; and to Mrs. William Sharp, Mrs. S. Masefield, Miss Littlejohn, Mrs. Stables, and Mr. Ben R. Streets for copies of unpublished poems by Lieut. Walter Lightowler Wilkinson, Acting-Captain Charles J. B. Masefield, Company Sergeant-Major W. H. Littlejohn, Lieut. J. Howard Stables, and Sergeant J. W. Streets. He is indebted to Mr. John Lane for permission to use some extracts from the letters in *Soldier and Dramatist*, by Harold Chapin, and to Messrs. Hodder and Stoughton for permission to use the extract from *Men of Letters*, by Dixon Scott. The list on pages 1-9 contains the titles of books of verse from which poetical extracts in this volume are taken, with names of their publishers.

A. St. J. A.

Soldier Poets who have fallen in the War

> To Odin's challenge we cried, Amen!
> We stayed the plough and laid by the pen
> And shouldered our guns like gentlemen,
> That the wiser weak should hold. . . .
>
> Then lift the flag of the Last Crusade,
> And fill the ranks of the Last Brigade!
> March on to the fields where the world's remade
> And the Ancient Dreams come true!
>   LIEUT. T. M. KETTLE, *Poems and Parodies.*

BRIAN BROOKE. Captain, 2nd Gordon Highlanders. (Fell in action, 1st July 1916. Died of wounds, 25th July.) *Poems.* With a Foreword by M. P. Willcocks (John Lane).

RUPERT BROOKE. Sub-Lieut. R.N.V.R. (Died on active service, 23rd April 1915.) *1914 and Other Poems; Collected Poems.* With Memoir (Sidgwick and Jackson).

LEONARD NIELL COOK, M.C. 2nd Lieut. Royal Lancs. Regt. (Killed in action, 7th July 1917.) *More Songs by the Fighting Men* (Erskine Macdonald).

A

LESLIE COULSON. Sergt. London Batt. Royal Fusiliers. (Killed in action, 7th October 1916.) *From an Outpost and Other Poems.* With Introduction by F. Raymond Coulson (Erskine Macdonald).

ARTHUR SCOTT CRAVEN (A. K. Harvey James). Captain, Buffs. (Killed in action, April 1917.) *Joe Skinner; Alarums and Excursions; The Last of the English* (Elkin Mathews); *A Fool's Tragedy.* A Novel (Martin Secker).

EUGENE CROMBIE. Captain, 4th Gordon Highlanders. (Killed in action, 23rd April 1917.) *More Songs by the Fighting Men* (Erskine Macdonald).

RICHARD DENNYS. Captain, Loyal North Lancs. Regt. (Wounded in Somme advance, 12th July 1916. Died, 24th July.) *There is No Death.* With Foreword by Captain Desmond Coke (John Lane).

HENRY LIONEL FIELD. Lieut. Royal Warwickshire Regt. (Killed in action, 1st July 1916.) *Poems and Drawings* (Birmingham : Cornish Bros.).

Soldier Poets

CLIFFORD FLOWER. Driver, Royal Field Artillery. (Killed in action, 20th April 1917.) *Memoir and Poems* (Privately printed).

HUGH REGINALD (REX) FRESTON. 2nd Lieut. 3rd Royal Berkshire Regt. (Killed in action, 24th January 1916.) *The Quest of Truth and Other Poems* (Oxford: Blackwell). *The Poetry of H. Rex Freston*, by Russell Markland (Ling).

The Hon. GERALD WILLIAM GRENFELL. Lieut. Rifle Brigade. (Killed in action, 30th July 1915.) *The Muse in Arms*. Edited by E. B. Osborn (John Murray).

The Hon. JULIAN GRENFELL, D.S.O. Captain, Royal Dragoons. (Wounded, 12th May 1915. Died, 26th May.) *Soldier Poets* (Erskine Macdonald). *Julian Grenfell*, by Viola Meynell (Burns and Oates).

WILLIAM NOEL HODGSON, M.C. Lieut. 9th Devon Regt. (Killed in action, 1st July 1916.) *Verse and Prose in Peace and War* (John Murray); *Soldier Poets* (Erskine Macdonald).

A. L. JENKINS. Lieut. R.F.C. (Killed in aeroplane accident, 31st December 1917.) *Forlorn Adventurers*. With Introduction by Frank Fletcher (Sidgwick and Jackson).

THOMAS M. KETTLE. Lieut. Dublin Fusiliers. (Killed in action, September 1916.) *Poems and Parodies*. With Preface by William Dawson (London: Duckworth. Dublin: Talbot Press). Prose: *The Ways of War* (Constable); *The Day's Burden* (Maunsel).

FRANCIS LEDWIDGE. Lance-Corpl. Inniskilling Fusiliers. (Killed in action, 1917.) *Songs of the Fields; Songs of Peace; Last Songs*. With Introductions by Lord Dunsany (Herbert Jenkins).

FRANK LEWIS. Flight Sub-Lieut. R.N.A.S. (Killed in air battle, 21st August 1917.) *More Songs by the Fighting Men* (Erskine Macdonald).

W. H. LITTLEJOHN. Company-Sergt.-Major, Middlesex Regt. (Killed in action, 10th April 1917.) *The Muse in Arms*. Edited by E. B. Osborn (John Murray).

Soldier Poets

EWART ALAN MACKINTOSH, M.C. Lieut. Seaforth Highlanders. (Killed in action, 21st November 1917.) *A Highland Regiment and Other Poems; War the Liberator and Other Pieces.* With Memoir by John Murray (John Lane).

HAMISH MANN. 2nd Lieut. Black Watch. (Wounded, 9th April 1917. Died, 10th April.) *A Subaltern's Musings* (John Long).

CHARLES JOHN BEECH MASEFIELD, M.C. Acting Captain, 5th North Staffs. Regt. (Fatally wounded in action, 1st July 1917. Died, a prisoner, 2nd July.) *The Seasons' Difference and Other Poems; Dislikes: Some Modern Satires* (Fifield); *More Songs by the Fighting Men* (Erskine Macdonald); *Gilbert Hermer*. A Novel (Blackwood).

COLIN MITCHELL. Sergt. Rifle Brigade. (Killed in action, 22nd March 1918.) *Trampled Clay* (Erskine Macdonald).

FRANCIS ST. VINCENT MORRIS. 2nd Lieut. 3rd Batt. Sherwood Foresters. Transferred R.F.C. (Died of wounds, 29th April 1917.) *Poems.* With a Memoir by L. A. G. S. (Oxford: Blackwell).

The Hon. ROBERT PALMER. Captain, Hants Regt. (Wounded on Tigris, 21st January 1916. Died, a prisoner in Turkish camp.) *The Muse in Arms.* Edited by E. B. Osborn (John Murray).

HAROLD PARRY. 2nd Lieut. 17th King's Royal Rifles. (Killed by shell, 6th May 1917.) *Letters and Poems.* With Memoir by G. P. D. (Walsall: W. H. Smith and Son).

The Hon. COLWYN ERASMUS ARNOLD PHILIPPS. Captain, Royal Horse Guards. (Killed in action, 13th May 1915.) *Poems and Letters* (John Murray).

A. VICTOR RATCLIFFE. Lieut. 10/13th West Yorks Regt. (Killed in action, 1st July 1916.) *Soldier Poets* (Erskine Macdonald).

ALEXANDER ROBERTSON. Corpl. 12th Yorks and Lancaster Regt. (Killed in action, 1st July 1916.) *Comrades; Last Poems* (Elkin Mathews).

GEORGE U. ROBINS. Captain, East Yorks Regt. (Killed in action, 5th May 1915.)

Lays of the Hertfordshire Hunt. With Preface by Major-Gen. Earl Cavan, and Memoir (A. L. Humphreys).

WILLIAM AMBROSE SHORT, C.M.G. Lieut.-Col. R.F.A. (Killed in action 21st June 1917.) *Poems* (A. L. Humphreys).

GEOFFREY BACHE SMITH. Lieut. Lancashire Fusiliers. (Killed in action, 3rd December 1916.) *A Spring Harvest* (Erskine Macdonald).

CHARLES HAMILTON SORLEY. Captain, Suffolk Regt. (Killed in action, 13th October 1915.) *Marlborough and Other Poems.* With Preface by W. R. S. (Cambridge University Press).

J. HOWARD STABLES. Lieut. Gurkha Rifles. (Wounded in action in Mesopotamia and missing, 17th February 1917. Since reported killed.) *The Sorrow that Whistled* (Elkin Mathews).

ROBERT W. STERLING. Lieut. Royal Scots Fusiliers. (Killed in action, 23rd April 1915.) *Poems.* With Memoir (Oxford University Press).

JOHN E. STEWART, M.C. Major, Staffordshire
Regt. (Killed in action, 26th April 1918.)
More Songs by the Fighting Men (Erskine
Macdonald).

JOHN WILLIAM STREETS. Sergt. 13th Yorks
and Lancaster Regt. (Wounded in action
and missing, 1st July 1916. Since reported
killed.) *The Undying Splendour* (Erskine
Macdonald).

The Hon. E. WYNDHAM TENNANT. Lieut.
Grenadier Guards. (Killed in action,
September 1915.) *Worple Flit and Other
Poems* (Oxford: Blackwell).

EDWARD THOMAS. Lieut. R.G.A. (Killed in
action, April 1917.) *Poems* (Selwyn and
Blount). Prose: *The Tenth Muse*. With
Memoir by John Freeman (Martin Secker);
A Literary Pilgrim in England (Methuen);
The Heart of England (Dent); *Rest and
Unrest* (Duckworth), etc.

HERBERT NICHOLAS TODD. Private, Queen's
Westminsters. (Killed in action, 7th October
1916.) *Poems and Plays* (Sedbergh: Jackson
and Son).

R. E. VERNEDE. Lieut. Rifle Brigade. (Killed
in action, 9th April 1917.) *War Poems*.

With Introduction by Edmund Gosse, C.B. (Heinemann). Prose: *Letters to His Wife*. With Introduction by C. H. Vernede (Collins); *The Pursuit of Mr. Faviel*. A Novel (Nelson), etc.

BERNARD CHARLES DE BOISMAISON WHITE. Lieut. 1st Tyneside Scottish Regt. (Killed in action, 1st July 1916.) *Remembrance and Other Verses*. With Memoir by V. Payne-Payne (Selwyn and Blount).

ERIC FITZWATER WILKINSON, M.C. Captain, West Yorkshire Regt. (Killed in action, 9th October 1917.) *Sunrise Dreams* (Erskine Macdonald); *Poet and Soldier*, by Fitzwater Wray; *Poetry Review* (Erskine Macdonald).

WALTER LIGHTOWLER WILKINSON. Lieut. 8th Argyll and Sutherland Highlanders. (Killed in action, 9th April 1917.) *More Songs by the Fighting Men* (Erskine Macdonald).

CYRIL W. WINTERBOTHAM. Lieut. Gloucestershire Regt. (Killed in action, 27th August 1916.) *Poems*. Published for private circulation. (Cheltenham: Banks and Son.) *The Muse in Arms*. Edited by E. B. Osborn (John Murray).

I

> Compare this England of to-day
> With England as she once has been.
> CAPT. C. H. SORLEY, *A Call to Action*.

HERE and there, in or near towns and villages all about these Islands, you will come upon public gardens and recreation grounds that, nowadays, are looking strangely desolate. One such garden, an old pleasaunce from which the noise of the city is walled out, lies near the centre of London, and I cannot pass it now without an impulse to bare my head. There is no grass on the wide lawn that in other years was trim and green. It has been worn away by the feet of the myriad young recruits I have seen training there in successive companies, some in khaki, some still in civilian dress, since the first days of the war; and the quiet, flower-bordered space is as black and bare to-day as if no grass had ever grown over it. The feet that have trodden it so have toiled

BRIAN BROOKE.
CAPTAIN, 2ND GORDON HIGHLANDERS.

since through the mud of France and Flanders, or the sands of Palestine or Mesopotamia, or up the rugged steeps of Gallipoli, and too many of them shall never take the way homeward any more. Our hearts know what these barren patches mean, for the shadow of their barrenness falls far across the lives we live. Some day the grass will grow again and happiness return to some of us, but there is too much gone that can never return.

Yet in our hearts, too, we know on an afterthought, that

> Nothing is here for tears, nothing to wail
> Or knock the breast —nothing but well and fair,
> And what may quiet us in a death so noble.

These men, these boys, who died that Freedom might live and that the higher hopes of mankind should not be trampled under by the lower, knew why they made the great sacrifice, and made it willingly in such a cause. And it is part of our pride in them that in this they have done nothing new, have taken no new way, but have trodden instinctively and worthily in a beaten track ; their courage, chivalry, love of justice, are theirs by inheritance, the ideals that led them are the common ideals that have led the best of our race through the past. So much you may learn by reading in the books that have been written by many soldier authors who have fought in this war and revealed in their verse or prose the faith and spirit that prompted them and their comrades-in-arms ; and, since it is still true that the soul of a nation lives in its literature, we shall understand them better, perhaps, and see how indissolubly they are linked up with the old traditions of our people, if we look back a little before we go farther.

It is curious to note that some contemporary enthusiasts speak and write of the democratic feeling which has broadened and deepened among us in these days as if it were a quite modern, rather sudden growth—a brand new spirit of common brotherhood that had been called into existence by the exigencies of the war. For most of us know it is merely the coming to full tide of the mighty undercurrent that has been slowly gathering force in our life, as in our literature, all down the centuries. You may catch sounds of it in Chaucer, a fuller music of it in Langland; and thenceforward, to Morris, Browning, Tennyson, Swinburne, and our soldier authors of to-day, there is scarcely a poet of any significance who does not more or less preach that simple gospel of humanity. Nor are these apostles of democracy to be set aside as discontented plebeians. The courtly Gascoigne, passionately denouncing social wrongs and inequalities and urging the duty of man to his fellows—

> O Knights, O Squires, O Gentle bloods yborn,
> You were not born all only for yourselves—

was as fine a democrat in the sixteenth century as Shelley was in the nineteenth. There are as true and trenchant things said for democracy in Sir Thomas More's *Utopia* as in the books of such moderns as Ruskin, Dickens, Carlyle, Wells, Shaw; and it is no stranger that our people should have risen spontaneously now for an ideal that is so literally in their blood, than that they should have put off the mild habits of civilian life and become instantly as hardy, fearless, and chivalrous soldiers as any in the world's history, for these qualities also are in their birthright.

We are accustomed to being patronised as an unimaginative race, in spite of the fact that no country has produced a greater imaginative literature. We are accustomed to being classed as a nation of shopkeepers, and have accepted the description indifferently, for it is not as if we had been accused of limiting our business activities to a single trade and (emulating the peculiar Prussian aspiration) of transforming ourselves into a nation of butchers. When you think of it, we actually are shopkeepers, in the large, sane meaning of the term, nor is it anyway to our discredit, so long as we make it clear, as we are doing again, that our honour is not of the things we sell.

Even Shakespeare was a shopkeeper, an unusually capable one ; and his partnership in a successful theatrical business did not prevent him from being a greater poet than any who never soiled his hands in a shop. A peaceful, useful occupation, shopkeeping in general is easily compatible with the pursuit of culture, with the living of that finer life of the spirit which differentiates the civilised man from the crude savage whose staple industry is war. It is a barbaric folk who, though there is no battle toward, delight in being soldiers all the time and accentuating the symbols of their profession. Those who have emerged from barbarism do not cease to be fighting men because they have ceased to be fighting men only. America and France are demonstrating that, and for ourselves—there is not more than an infinitesimal part of our army that knew how to handle a gun before this war was declared, and it was significant of our small professional army that, so far from loving to clothe itself in extravagant terrors, its officers made it almost a point of etiquette to get out of uniform into mufti whenever they were off duty. I think the native common sense of the shopkeeping Britisher brought him long since to see the absurdity of the cult of militarism, the childishness of cultivating ferocious moustaches and wearing spiked helmets in order to look dangerous. That sort of thing, which passes in Germany as impressive and up-to-date, is ridiculously behind the times. They know better even in China than to cling any longer to a hope of being able to

Photo by Maull & Fox.

THE HON. JULIAN GRENFELL, D.S.O.
CAPTAIN, ROYAL DRAGOONS.

Soldier Poets

terrify their opponents by wearing ugly masks. Another point in our favour, as a civilised race, is that we do not and never did devote our energies to acquiring the goose-step. Like sensible people we are contented to leave that style of locomotion to the bird that is naturally afflicted with it.

Anyhow, those manifestations of raw barbarism are obsolete; they are signs, in a modern community, of moral and mental degeneracy. German professors have confidently written us down as degenerates because the passion for militarism, the lust for conquest, has departed from us, and we are no longer moved to spend our lives in swaggering about in battle array, rattling sharp swords and truculently menacing the goods and lives of our neighbours. But I prefer to believe that since we became a lettered, cultured country we have lost the taste for blood, and that the arrogant exhibition of courage has never entered into our conception of the competent, heroic warrior.

For the last seven centuries which of our poets who have themselves been soldiers have blustered of their brute strength or eulogised the glory of war? Though Chaucer fought against France under Edward III. and tells in gallant fashion of tilt and tourney and the high doings of chivalry, there is little that is martial in his poetry. You remember the Knight in his *Canterbury Tales*—how he had proved himself 'full worthy' in war; had for his puissance been placed at table above the knights of every other country; yet as his crowning praise Chaucer chronicles it that, though brave, he was wise,

> And of his port as meek as is a maid.
> He never yet no villainy ne said
> In all his life unto no manner wight:
> He was a very perfect gentle knight.

Moreover, into his conception of the

Temple of Mars the father of English poetry puts nothing of that pride and splendour of war which might be supposed to appeal to a soldier poet of his earlier day: it is a 'sory place,' he says, and the paintings on its walls are all of murder, assassinations, 'open warres,' with bleeding wretches in agony, and in the midst sits Mischance,

> With sory comfort and evil countenance.

True, there is a figure of Conquest painted up in a tower, but as he sits with a sword suspended above him by a single thread, it is not to be presumed that his position is worth occupying.

There is nothing whatever in the verse of the Earl of Surrey to remind you that he went fighting in France. Sir Walter Raleigh, that daring, dashing hero, never fought with his pen: all his poems are of an amatory, philosophical, or pleasantly pastoral order. And Sir Philip Sidney, our ideal soldier, made no song that boasts of his prowess or triumphs over his enemies, but wrote the loveliest sonnets to the moon, to sleep, to love, and verses that sigh over the vanity of human things. These, and other of our soldier poets like them, dead and living, seem to be a vastly different type of fighting man from the ' blonde beast,' the professional slaughterer adored of the German intellectuals, and this war is showing and will show which of the two types is fittest to survive in a reasonable world, and which belongs to the jungle and is doomed to extinction.

Two hundred years after Chaucer was dead, you find his ideal of the British soldier persisting (for it was the national ideal) in Ben Jonson's epistle ' to a friend, Master Colby, to persuade him to the wars '—an appeal that might well have been written yesterday, so applicable is it to what is happening in our generation :—

Wake, friend, from forth thy lethargy : the drum
Beats brave and loud in Europe, and bids come
All that dare rouse, or are not loath to quit
Their vicious ease and be o'erwhelmed with it.
It is a call to keep the spirits alive
That gasp for action and would yet revive
Man's buried honour in his sleepy life,
Quickening dead nature to her noblest strife. . . .

Go, quit them all, and take along with thee
Thy true friend's wishes, Colby, which shall be
That thine be just and honest, that thy deeds
Not wound thy conscience when thy body bleeds ;
That thou dost all things more for truth than glory,
And never but for doing wrong be sorry ;
That by commanding first thyself thou mak'st
Thy person fit for any charge thou tak'st ;
That fortune never make thee to complain,
But what she gives thou dare give her again ;
That whatsoever face thy fate puts on
Thou shrink nor start not, but be always one ;
That thou think nothing great but what is good,
And from that thought strive to be understood.
So, 'live or dead, thou wilt preserve a fame
Still precious with the odour of thy name ;
And last, blaspheme not ; we did never hear
Man thought the valianter 'cause he durst swear.
These take, and now go seek thy peace in war :
Who falls for love of God shall rise a star.

Ben was no milk-and-water poet either. In his youth he fought with our armies in Flanders; he was not without experience of war, and you may take it he was addressing, in Master Colby, the type of Englishman who shattered the pride of the Spanish Armada, who wrought on the same field as Sidney—men who went into battle not as ravening brutes lusting to befoul any victory they won by a savage slaughter of children and women and defenceless civilians, but as free, clean human creatures, prepared to take arms and slay or be slain, in fair fight with armed men, for a cause they felt to be just, and yet in the hour of triumph

> By objects which might force the soul to abate
> Her feeling, rendered more compassionate.

Pass over another two centuries, and the same national ideal of the British soldier survives still inviolate in Tennyson's 'Ode on the Death of the Duke of Wellington':—

> Yet remember all
> He spoke among you, and the Man who spoke;
> Who never sold the truth to serve the hour,
> Nor paltered with eternal God for power;
> Who never spoke against a foe;
> Whose eighty winters freeze with one rebuke
> All great self-seekers trampling on the right;
> Truth-teller was our English Alfred named;
> Truth-lover was our English Duke;
> Whatever record leap to light,
> He never shall be shamed.

The same ideal of the great soldier recurs again and again to-day in the songs of our soldier poets, for it is the racial tradition in which they and their comrades grew up while they were men of peace, and inevitably it fashioned them in its likeness when they became soldiers themselves.

Certainly, some little has been written in praise of war by some of our last century authors who had only seen it from a distance—they were reconciled to it because they imagined it had regenerating influences on mankind, that it gave fresh impetus to commercial enterprise and fostered the arts. There may be a sediment of truth in this; but with equal truth you might say as much of religion. Ruskin considered it a subtle testimony to this influence that spears, shields, helmets, implements of warfare, were lovingly and richly enchased with artistic decorations, whilst no man was moved to carve images of beauty on his spade or on the handles of his plough. But whatever significance lay in these facts belongs to the past; it is in the same sense significant that nothing could be more severely unadorned than the modern cannon, rifle, or machine-gun. In sober earnest, we have arrived at a recognition of war as nothing but a necessary and degrading evil in the human community, and as not the less evil for being still necessary. Men of reason face it now precisely as they face the need of forming a rescue party to descend into a burning mine or to launch a lifeboat into the blind fury of

Photo by Langfier.

W. N. HODGSON, M.C.
LIEUT., DEVON REGIMENT.

a storm—unafraid, but not glorying. There are, of course, exceptions among us, but as a nation we have arrived at years of discretion; we have outgrown that pride in the exhibition of muscular superiority over our neighbours which is pardonable, though silly enough, in youth, but a sign of madness in maturity; and it would not have been possible to rouse any enthusiasm in this country to-day for an aggressive or unjustified war. Our friends and fellow-workers have armed in their millions, not because they love 'the sport of kings,' or because they thirst for glory, or domination, or booty; but because they realise that there is no other way of saving their own souls and the soul of the world from being cast into a primitive hell upon earth with an All-Highest War Lord on the throne of it and his two-headed Kultur at the gate; and because, at the outset, their manhood and their honour would not let them turn a deaf ear to the agony of outraged Belgium. The cry of that agony came to all of us with the compelling force that is in Cromwell's poignant appeal to the French king, when the Piedmontese, whom France was pledged to protect, were ruthlessly massacred by their oppressors :—

'There are reasons of State which might give thee inducement not to reject these People of the Valleys flying for shelter to thee: but I would not have thee, so great a king as thou art, be moved to the defence of the unfortunate by other reasons than the promise of thy Ancestors and thy own piety and royal benignity and greatness of mind. So shall the praise and fame of this most worthy action be unmixed and clear, and thyself shalt find the Father of Mercy and his Son Christ, whose name and doctrine thou shalt have vindicated, the more favourable to thee and propitious through the course of thy life.'

It is some such high cause as this, such principles and emotions as these that give war nearly all the poetry and the glory that can ever be found in it. There is nothing of either in the mere exhibition of military might, the boast of conquest, the raw carnage, the hecatombs of slain. Something magnificent there is, apart from every ethical consideration, in all heroic fighting against odds, in any act of supreme courage on the field, in so desperate a charge as that of the Light Brigade at Balaclava, in the deathless story of the great retreat from Mons, even if you forget the cause for which those heroes fell. But probably the incidents that uplift us most in the telling are incidents in which the kindly, self-sacrificing instincts of men are seen to survive amidst the barbarity and indescribable inferno of a battlefield. The dying Sidney's ready compassion for the soldier who lay wounded beside him at Zutphen, his simple self-renunciatory 'His need is greater than mine,' are worth nearly all his poetry.

The right touch, too, is in each of those innumerable tales of how on a stricken field a soldier will turn aside under a hail of bullets to carry a wounded comrade into safety. It is in countless records of the present war: in the narrative of how the men of a British battery were shattered and decimated till only three remained, and these three, wounded as they were, worked the last gun unflinchingly until relief could be sent to them; in that of how a retiring troop of war-worn Britishers handed their rations over to starving refugees; in that of how, whenever our seamen sink the enemy's ships they promptly lower their boats to save the drowning Huns. And see how finely a stray act of German chivalry can shine out against the black record her hordes have elsewhere made for themselves. Somewhere along the Marne, a French sergeant and two hundred men were cut off from their regiment and surrounded. They held their ground till every man of them was killed or wounded; then when the victors swept in upon them the German commander saluted the French sergeant and was so keen to honour his bravery that he had him carried from the place with his rifle lying beside him on the stretcher. A trifle, no doubt; but there is a very different light about it from that which haloes the ruins of Louvain and the murder of Captain Fryatt.

I have known many who voluntarily abandoned a pleasant life and golden prospects for the future, as soon as the war came upon us, to fight for freedom and human rights, from nothing but an irresistible sense of duty and honour. I have stood at railway stations and seen our soldiers—who had been clerks and artisans a few months before—set out for the front stoically or cheerily, and have noted how their womenfolk, gathered to see them off, have heartened them with smiling good-byes, and only broken into tears when the train had carried their men beyond sight of their weakness. I have stood at railway stations and seen tired and muddied soldiers from the trenches coming home on leave, and here and there from the vast crowd outside a mother, a father, a wife, a child, a sister, a brother, a sweetheart, run forward with sudden outcries to get a hold on this or that one of them, and the two go off crying and laughing together. I have seen the wounded coming out from those stations and men among the patient crowd without standing bareheaded or stirred to sudden cheering as they passed, and women who stepped into the road to fling flowers upon the bandaged, recumbent figures inside the ambulances. And I have a vivid memory of seeing a regiment of Scots Guards tramping along Cannon Street from the Tower to Waterloo Station, in the days when the war was still new and strange to us. A sturdy, martial body of men, they marched with their band playing, rank after rank, four deep, and in such numbers that the band had gone on beyond hearing in the traffic before the last of them went by me ; and most vividly of all it comes back to me of how at intervals a wife, a sweetheart, a mother, or a friend marched with certain of the soldiers. Particularly I remember one bronzed guardsman, a handsome, well-set-up fellow, who went a little out of the line to make room betwixt himself and his khakied neighbour for a fatherly, grey-bearded civilian who had shouldered the guardsman's rifle so as to leave him free to carry his little girl, a child of two, whilst his wife, with a tremulous smile about her lips, kept pace with him, linked to his arm. The homeliness of that group in so warlike a setting helped to illustrate in its way, as those other memories do in theirs, all that I have been labouring here to express : that all the good and gracious human qualities in men are formed and nurtured in peace, amidst the decencies of common, everyday life; that war may on occasion evoke them, but it no more creates them than the night creates the stars.

II

War is declared in Britain, such is the news and true;
Now that the mother's smitten, what will her litters do?
Volunteers, all come forward, stand to your arms like men,
Let the Germans know that where'er they go,
If at home or here, they will meet their foe
When they come to the Mother's den.
        CAPT. BRIAN BROOKE, *Only a Volunteer*.

BEFORE Armageddon was upon us, then, and the old world came to an end, we used to say that all our war songs were written by soft-handed civilians who were never under fire; and this was true enough when we said it, but is true no longer. In the past, the poets seldom became soldiers. When they did they saw too much of what lay behind the glory of war to make any songs about it. No soldier, but the scholarly poet-antiquary, Michael Drayton, enriched our literature with the vigorous, triumphant 'Ballad of Agincourt'; it was the snug civilian

Campbell who sang the most bellicose and immortal lyrics on our naval victories; the recluse dreamer, Tennyson, who thrilled us with ' The Charge of the Light Brigade ' —indeed, he and the even less soldierly Swinburne gave militant patriotism the noblest utterance it has achieved since Shakespeare, another man of peace, voiced it in proud phrases that stir the old Adam in us still like the sound of a trumpet.

Since August 1914, however, a new world and a new order of things have been rising out of a new chaos. Civilian poets have been writing memorable songs of this war, but not often in the old mood. What was a minor strain in the war verse of Napoleonic and Crimean years (it is in some of Byron's and Coleridge's poems and, later and more poignantly, in Sydney Dobell's ' England in Time of War ') has persisted until it is the major theme of the civilian and soldier war poetry of to-day. The fighting men are no longer contented to be dumb pawns in a game; they no longer remain silent of their own experiences and ideals; no longer leave inexperienced civilian singers to paint fancy pictures of battle and interpret their thoughts and emotions for them. They have stripped the thing of its gaudy trappings, they have bared their own hearts to us, and we know that they are speaking now not for themselves only, but for our armies and our nation as a whole. For when the Hun, mad for power, started to run amok through human rights and the sanities of civilisation, and the young manhood of our race spontaneously rose to answer that challenge, they were of all sorts and conditions who swarmed to the recruiting stations—aristocrats and navvies, artisans and university professors, tradesmen, farmers, lawyers, stockbrokers, actors, artists, and poets—and these last, drawn also from every grade of society, have coalesced into a representative group which is of itself a sort of microcosm of our army, as our army is of our nation.

Before the war, Rupert Brooke had won the Rugby school prize for his poem, 'The Bastille,' gained a Fellowship at King's, Cambridge, and was devoting himself to scholarship and literature; Francis Ledwidge had been a scavenger on the roads of Ireland; Edward Thomas was already a distinguished critic and essayist; Hugh Reginald Freston was at Oxford reading for his B.A. degree; John William Streets was a Derbyshire miner, striving for self-culture and writing verse in his leisure; while the Hon. Julian Grenfell and his brother, the Hon. Gerald, the Hon. E. Wyndham Tennant, the Hon. Robert Palmer (brother of Viscount Wolmer), and the Hon. Colwyn Philipps, born and bred in far other circumstances, were as ready to sacrifice all that was theirs in the common cause. Leslie Coulson was a brilliant young London journalist; Charles

Hamilton Sorley was fresh from Marlborough; R. E. Vernede was a successful novelist; Nicholas Todd was a schoolmaster; Clifford Flower a clerk to an iron and steel manufacturer; Alexander Robertson a lecturer on history at Sheffield University; Arthur Scott Craven had made a reputation as an actor in London and America, had published a play, two volumes of verse, and a novel of considerable power; Henry Field was an art student; John E. Stewart, the son of working-class parents, was a school teacher; Charles Masefield, a cousin of John Masefield, was a lawyer; Francis St. Vincent Morris had entered his name on the books of Wadham, Oxford, but went from Brighton College, when the war came, to take a commission in the Sherwood Foresters; Bernard de Boismaison White had been on the staff of a London publishing house and in the publicity department of the Marconi Company; Thomas Kettle was an Irish barrister and a professor at Dublin University; Richard Dennys had taken his M.R.C.S. and L.R.C.P. degrees, but never practised—he was in Florence when war was declared, 'working with Gordon Craig at his school for the improvement of the Art of the Theatre,' and at once returned to England, and was gazetted to a regiment of the line.

One might go on, and having completed this list of the homeland's soldier poets who have been killed in action, add to it an even longer list of such poets who are still in the fighting line (I am saying nothing here of the many, their peers in song as in arms, from the Britains overseas), and you would discover that, till the German onslaught left them no honourable choice, they were, with one or two exceptions, essentially men of peace—they belonged to or were preparing for almost any trade or profession but that of the soldier. They were the true pacifists, so sincere in their devotion to Peace that they did not hesitate to fight and die for her sake; they were the authentic conscientious objectors, loathing bloodshed, yet ready to shed their own in safeguarding others who were dear to them, not afraid to put aside private scruples and, in a spirit of self-abnegation, to risk losing their personal souls that the freedom of the world and the general soul of the race might be saved.

In saying this I am not trying my hand at rhetorical flourishes; I am merely summarising, as best I may, the gospel, the ideals, the aspirations that are enshrined in their war poetry. There is a wide world of difference between those romantic old war lyrics that our patriotic civilians used to write and the grim realism or high spiritual significances of those that were written in the mud and squalor of the trenches, in dug-out or billet, just before going into action, just after coming out of it, in the quiet of a rest-camp or while their writers were lying wounded in hospital. No Hymn of Hate is among them, no glorification of slaughter, no note of boastfulness or blatancy, but a deep love of country, a clear, rational sense of the tragedy and dire necessity of what must be done, in such an hour as this, by all who value liberty and honour more than peace at the price of both, an unwavering vision of the end to be fought for, faith in God and in each other, with those qualities of self-sacrifice and heroic resolve that you would look for in men who had rallied to what they were determined should be a last crusade against the folly and crime of war, and had gone forth together on that knightly quest, following the Holy Grail of a great ideal.

There are inevitable contrasts in the appeal of war to the man who became a soldier from natural inclination, and the man who never would have adopted that

FRANCIS LEDWIDGE.
LANCE-CORPL., INNISKILLING FUSILIERS.

profession from choice and did so only in a crisis and from a deliberate realisation of patriotic or altruistic duty. Both live and die by the same code of chivalry, honour, indomitable courage, for our New Army has grown up in the proud traditions of the Old. Given a cause worth defending, the one goes eagerly into battle, berserker-like, for the sheer joy of it. The other goes with equal readiness, pluck and grim purpose, feels the same fierce joy of it in the heat of conflict, but in his before and after thoughts cannot so stoically away with doubts and compunctions.

The two types have their spokesmen among the poets who have fallen in this war. The Old Army speaks through Captain Brian Brooke and Captain Julian Grenfell; the soul of the New Army reveals itself in the songs of a multitude of singers.

Brian Brooke was a born soldier. He

came of a notable fighting stock; his father and two brothers were in the Army, and two other brothers had entered the Navy. From his childhood he revelled in tales of military prowess; 'his greatest longing had always been to be a soldier,' we are told; but his sight was defective and he could not pass the medical examination. Making the best of his disappointment, he went to British East Africa, won the adoration of the natives by his good comradeship and boundless daring, and grew famous there as a big game hunter. The outbreak of war gave him his opportunity, and he fought as a trooper in the British East African Force. But news that his brother had been killed in action in Flanders brought him home, and he succeeded in getting gazetted captain in his brother's regiment, the Gordon Highlanders. 'He refused a good appointment on the staff of the force then advancing into German East Africa,' says

M. P. Willcocks, 'went to France early in 1916, and within three weeks was commanding in the Great Push at Mametz, on 1st July. Twice wounded, he still led his men over two lines of German trenches, but at the third fell, torn with terrible wounds, and died after three weeks of agony, his sole regret being that he could not go back to his troops.'

This is the man as he discloses himself in his book—an ardent, downright man of action, full-blooded, intensely alive, simple, honourable, likeable, not troubled overmuch with brooding introspection and the pale cast of thought, but rich in a rugged, common-sense philosophy and a breezy humanity that find outlets in his stirring ballads of hunting, fighting, and adventure. Danger and hardship exhilarated him; he would risk his life in a gamble as keenly as others risk their money. When we were struggling desperately against the first gigantic onrush of the enemy, and voluntary recruiting here was in full swing, he was scathingly contemptuous of

> The courage of the dauntless few who dared to stay behind;

and into one verse of 'A Father's Advice' he has condensed his soldierly creed—which is the creed, after all, of our Armies both New and Old:

> Never look for Strife, he's an ugly brute,
>   But meet him whenever and where he likes;
> Only draw your gun when you mean to shoot,
>   And strike as long as your enemy strikes.
> Never force a fight on a smaller man,
>   Nor turn your back on a stronger clown.
> Keep standing as long as you darned well can,
>   And fight like the devil when once you're down!

The dogged heart of the Old Contemptibles is in that: it was so they quitted them on the Great Retreat, and made defeat as glorious as a victory.

In Julian Grenfell, eldest son of Lord Desborough, the characteristic qualities of the old and new soldier met and were reconciled. He passed from Eton and

Oxford, four years before the war, to take a commission in the Dragoons. Delighting in the profession of arms, he was also something of a visionary, a mystic, and when he came to write of battle and death transfigured them to shapes of spiritual loveliness. 'He had,' says Miss Viola Meynell, ' such shining qualities of youth, such strength and courage and love, that to others who are young he seems like the perfection of themselves. They know so well day by day just what their own youth can fall to and rise to; and it is when their youth rises most, to its utmost fierceness and tenderness, that they come near to him, who was made of those things.' He and Charles Lister were friends; and not long before he also fell in battle, Lister wrote to his friend's mother, Lady Desborough, of the grief that unmanned him when he thought of Julian's death. 'I suppose everybody noted dear Julian's vitality,' he adds, 'but I don't think they were so conscious of that great tenderness of heart that underlay it. He always showed it most with you; and with women generally it was his special charm. . . . I remember a time when he was under the impression that I'd chucked Socialism for the " loaves and fishes," etc. etc.; and of course that sort of thing he couldn't abide, and he thought this for a longish while; then found out that it wasn't that after all, and took my hand in his in the most loving way.' He goes on to recall Julian Grenfell's moral courage, his physical bravery, his passionate search for truth, and ' what an ardent love he had for honesty of purpose, and intellectual honesty, and what sacrifices he made for them; and sacrifices of peace of mind abhorrent to most Englishmen.'

All which squares with the casual self-revelations in letters he wrote home while he was on service in India and Africa:

'I hate material books centred on whether people are successful. I like books about artists and philosophers and dreamers, and anybody who is a little off his dot.' 'I agree with what you say about success, but I like the people best who take it as it comes, or doesn't come, and are busy about unpractical and ideal things in their heart of hearts all the time.' 'I am so happy here. I love the Profession of Arms, and I love my fellow officers, and all my dogs and all my horses.' Later, from Flanders, he wrote that he longed to be able to say he liked what he was going through there: 'But it's beastly. I pretended to myself for a bit that I liked it, but it was no good, it only made me careless and unwatchful and self-absorbed; but when one acknowledged to oneself that it *was* beastly, one became all right again, and cool.' Again, writing from the front of the hard times he was enduring, 'It is all *the* best of fun,' he said. 'I have never, never felt so well, or so happy, or enjoyed anything so much. The fighting excitement vitalises everything, every sight and word and action.'

There are unforgettable stories of his gallantry on the day when he was mortally wounded. He volunteered to carry a message through to the front line, and got there and back under heavy fire. As he rejoined his General on a hill, he was struck in the head by a shell splinter, and said as he lay bleeding, ' Go down, sir, don't bother about me. I'm done.' The General helped to carry him down, and Grenfell told a brother officer, ' Do you know, I think I shall die,' and being contradicted said quietly, ' Well, you see if I don't ! ' At the dressing-station he asked for the truth, saying, ' I only want to know. I'm not in the least afraid.' A fortnight after, on the 26th May 1915, he died of his wound—only two months before his younger brother, Lieutenant

THE HON. E. WYNDHAM TENNANT.
LIEUT., GRENADIER GUARDS.
(From a Portrait by SARGENT)

Gerald William Grenfell, a gracious spirit loving ' whatsoever things are fair ' (to apply to himself a phrase from his lines on the death of a friend), was killed in action.

Early in May 1915 Julian Grenfell had sent home to his friends his one great poem, ' Into Battle,' which in character and temperament chimes perfectly with what Charles Lister wrote of him, and with what we learn of him from his letters :

> The naked earth is warm with Spring,
>   And with green grass and bursting trees
> Leans to the sun's gaze glorying,
>   And quivers in the sunny breeze.
> And Life is Colour and Warmth and Light,
>   And a striving evermore for these ;
> And he is dead who will not fight,
>   And who dies fighting has increase.
>
> The fighting man shall from the sun
>   Take warmth, and life from the glowing earth,
> Speed with the light-foot winds to run,
>   And with the trees to newer birth,
> And find, when fighting shall be done,
>   Great rest, and fullness after dearth. . . .

In dreary, doubtful, waiting hours,
   Before the brazen frenzy starts,
The horses show him nobler powers:
   O patient eyes, courageous hearts!

And when the burning moment breaks,
   And all things else are out of mind,
And only joy of battle takes
   Him by the throat and makes him blind—

Through joy and blindness he shall know,
   Not caring much to know, that still
Nor lead nor steel can reach him, so
   That it be not the destined Will.

The thundering line of battle stands,
   And in the air death moans and sings,
But day shall clasp him with strong hands,
   And night shall fold him in soft wings.

The difference of attitude and feeling in the new soldier, who became a soldier not from predilection, but against it and from a sheer sense of duty, is manifest at once, I think, in the 'Before Battle' of W. N. Hodgson, the third and youngest son of the Bishop of St. Edmundsbury and

Ipswich. In March 1913 he took a First Class in Classical Moderations at Oxford; next year, in the first days of the war, he obtained a commission in the 9th Devon Regiment. He was mentioned in despatches, and in October 1915 the Military Cross was conferred upon him; on the 1st July 1916 he fell in the battle of the Somme. There is strength and spiritual and emotional beauty in his verse and that air of plain sincerity which distinguishes all these poets who were soldiers. At least two or three of his poems will have an abiding place in all war anthologies, and one of such must assuredly be his ' Before Battle ' :

> By all the glories of the day
>   And the cool evening's benison ;
> By the last sunset touch that lay
>   Upon the hills when day was done ;
> By beauty lavishly outpoured,
>   And blessings carelessly received,
>   By all the days that I have lived,
> Make me a soldier, Lord.

> By all of all men's hopes and fears,
>   And all the wonders poets sing,
> The laughter of unclouded years,
>   And every sad and lovely thing :
> By the romantic ages stored
>   With high endeavour that was his
>   By all his sad catastrophes,
> Make me a man, O Lord.
>
> I, that on my familiar hill
>   Saw with uncomprehending eyes
> A hundred of Thy sunsets spill
>   Their fresh and sanguine sacrifice,
> Ere the sun swings his noonday sword
>   Must say good-bye to all of this :
>   By all delights that I shall miss,
> Help me to die, O Lord.

The sturdy, sober courage of this matches Grenfell's brave ecstasy. The difference between them is only of tone and temperament—the same fighting blood is in each, as it was in the long-ago Cavalier and Roundhead. Maybe it is that our race is compact of these two elements; the Cavalier and Roundhead have intermarried and are inextricably mixed in us all, but in very varying proportions. They came near, perhaps, to striking a balance in Rupert Brooke. He responded so instantly to 'the call' that he was a sub-lieutenant in the Royal Navy in September 1914, and in October took part in the Antwerp expedition. His greeting of the war shouts in that first of his sonnets, ' Peace,' with all the exultation that is in Grenfell's lines, but not because he foretasted the joy of battle. He was supremely satisfied because he felt that in the years of peace our souls had put on too much flesh; we had become gross and sordid and forgotten our ideals, and now the war had suddenly uplifted us from the slough, restored our manhood to us and touched us to noble issues :

Now, God be thanked Who has matched us with
    His hour
  And caught our youth and wakened us from
    sleeping,
With hand made sure, clear eye, and sharpened
    power

To turn, as swimmers into cleanness leaping,
Glad from a world grown old and cold and weary.
　Leave the sick hearts that honour could not move,
And half-men, and their dirty songs and dreary,
　And all the little emptiness of love. . . .

And again there is this rush of joyance in his rapturous requiem :

Blow out, you bugles, over the rich Dead!
　There's none of these so lonely and poor of old
　But, dying, has made us rarer gifts than gold. . . .
Blow, bugles, blow! They brought us, for our dearth,
　Holiness, lacked so long, and Love and Pain.
Honour has come back, as a king, to earth,
　And paid his subjects with a royal wage ;
And Nobleness walks in our ways again ;
　And we have come into our heritage.

Rupert Brooke was almost the first of these soldier poets to give up his life in his country's service. He had been no more than two months on duty with the Mediterranean Force when he died of blood-poisoning, on the 23rd April 1915, and was buried at Skyros.

III

> It is too late now to retrieve
> A fallen dream, too late to grieve
> A name unmade, but not too late
> To thank the gods for what is great :
> A keen-edged sword, a soldier's heart,
> Is greater than a poet's art,
> And greater than a poet's fame
> A little grave that has no name.
>   LANCE-CORPL. FRANCIS LEDWIDGE, *Last Songs*.

NONE of the poets of the New Armies has written finer poetry than Francis Ledwidge, and few have found less inspiration in the war itself. The first of his books, *Songs of the Fields*, made its appearance when the war was young and he was still a civilian; the second, which he named *Songs of Peace*, after he had put on khaki and was gone on active service. He fought on the Serbian Retreat, and in Gallipoli; then was sent to Flanders, where he fell in action in July 1917. 'I have taken up arms,' he wrote to Lord Dunsany, 'for the fields along the Boyne, and the birds and the blue sky over them '; and in that second book of his you see him moving through scenes of conflict in strange lands, but still dreaming and singing of home and the peace of home. Though his poems are divided into those written in barracks, in camp, at sea, in Serbia, in Greece, in hospital in Egypt, and again in barracks, there is not a war song among them. In barracks he sings of love, of May, of a place he knew in Ireland where the birds used to sing:

And when the war is over I shall take
My lute adown to it and sing again
Songs of the whispering things among the brake,
And those I love shall know them by their strain.
Their airs shall be the blackbird's twilight song,
Their words shall be all flowers with fresh dews
　　hoar—
But it is lonely now in winter long,
And, God, to hear the blackbird sing once more!

In camp and on the sea his verse is all of clouds, flowers, the sky and the trees

Photo by Elliott & Fry.

THE HON. COLWYN ERASMUS ARNOLD PHILIPPS.
CAPTAIN, ROYAL HORSE GUARDS.

and hills of Ireland; the hints of darker things are few and faint and elusive. In hospital his thoughts turn wistfully to Ireland, ' My Mother ' :

> God made my mother on an April day
> From sorrow and the mist along the sea,
> Lost birds' and wanderers' songs and ocean spray,
> And the moon loved her, wandering jealously. . . .
>
> Kind heart she has for all on hill or wave
> Whose hopes grew wings, like ants, to fly away.
> I bless the God Who such a mother gave
> This poor bird-hearted singer of a day.

The war makes only a pensive undertone even in 'Evening Clouds,' with its vision of Rupert Brooke's grave :

> A little flock of clouds go down to rest
> In some blue corner of the moon's highway,
> With shepherd winds that shook them in the west
> To borrowed shapes of earth in bright array,
> Perhaps to weave a rainbow's gay festoons
> Around the lonesome isle which Brooke has made
> A little England full of lovely noons,
> Or dot it with his country's mountain shade.

Ledwidge proved himself a doughty soldier; his heart was in the war, though the war was not in his heart—there was no room in that for anything but his love of home and the treasures of peace for which he was fighting. His Helicon, like the Kingdom of Heaven, was within him; he drew most of his inspiration from his memories of Ireland, and there is no lyric in his *Songs of Peace* more exquisite in feeling and utterance than 'A Little Boy in the Morning '—

> He will not come, and still I wait.
> He whistles at another gate
> Where angels listen. Ah, I know
> He will not come, yet if I go,
> How shall I know he did not pass
> Barefooted in the flowery grass ? . . .

The war breaks in upon the music of his *Last Songs* now and then, but more often these poems written in France or Belgium are of nothing but flowers and fairies, birds and children and the sights and

Francis Ledwidge 59

sounds of his own land, for, as his little song ' In France ' has it—

> Whatever way I turn I find
> The path is old unto me still ;
> The hills of home are in my mind,
> And there I wander as I will.

There is enough, and more than enough, in his three volumes to indicate what our literature has lost by his early death and to justify Lord Dunsany, who discovered and fostered his genius and introduced his work to the world at large, in saying, ' I give my opinion that if Ledwidge had lived, this lover of all the seasons in which the blackbird sings would have surpassed even Burns, and Ireland would have lawfully claimed, as she may even yet, the greatest of peasant singers.'

The mental detachment that characterised Ledwidge, the readiness to escape in hours of leisure from his grim, abnormal surroundings into an atmosphere that was native to him, characterises the verse in

Wyndham Tennant's one small volume, *Worple Flit and Other Poems*. A lieutenant of the Grenadiers, he fell in battle on the Somme at the age of nineteen—one year older than Chatterton. He passed the proofs of his book on the eve of the attack in which he was to die, and finished a last letter that night to his mother, Lady Glenconner, with the quotation that he uses on his title page :

High heart, high speech, high deeds, 'mid honouring eyes.

He so literally lisped in numbers that he used to dictate quaint little poems even before he could write. One that he addressed to his mother when he was eight years old is full of his love and admiration of her put into most childishly simple terms, with here and there a touch that flashes into sudden beauty :

> . . . She is full of love and grace,
> A kind of flower in all the place. . . .

Wyndham Tennant

> Even the trees give her salutes,
> They seem to know who's near their
>   roots. . . .
> She is something quite divine,
> And joy, oh joy, this mother's mine.

Two of the poems in his volume were written whilst he was at Winchester College, but the rest are dated from shell-shattered towns, whose names have become almost household words to us, and the war but rarely and intermittently intrudes into them. The longest, 'The Nightingale,' a glamorous love story adapted from Boccaccio, was written at Ypres and Poperinghe during June and July 1916. At Ypres, Poperinghe, Ecques, and Hullach Road he wrote the fanciful, bizarre old-world ballads of 'Worple Flit' and 'The Knight and the Russet Palmer'; some thoughtful lines on reincarnation, and a song or two in lighter moods. When the war does enter into his verse, as in 'Home Thoughts in Laventie,' it comes somewhat as a wonderful dream-pedlar, bringing dreams that are not of itself :

> Green gardens in Laventie !
>   Soldiers only know the street
> Where the mud is churned and splashed about
>   By battle-wending feet ;
> And yet beside one stricken house there is a glimpse of grass,
>   Look for it when you pass.
>
> Beyond the church whose pitted spire
>   Seems balanced on a strand
> Of swaying stone and tottering brick
>   Two roofless ruins stand.
> And here behind the wreckage where the back wall should have been
>   We found a garden green. . . .
>
> So all among the vivid blades
>   Of soft and tender grass
> We lay, nor heard the limber wheels
>   That pass and ever pass
> In noisy continuity, until their stony rattle
>   Seems in itself a battle.
>
> At length we rose up from this ease
>   Of tranquil, happy mind,

And searched the garden's little length
  A fresh pleasaunce to find ;
And there some yellow daffodils and jasmine hanging high
  Did rest the tired eye.

The fairest and most fragrant
  Of the many sweets we found
Was a little bush of Daphne flower
  Upon a grassy mound,
And so thick were the blossoms set and so divine the scent
  That we were well content.

Hungry for Spring I bent my head,
  The perfume fanned my face,
And all my soul was dancing
  In that little lovely place,
Dancing with a measured step from wrecked and shattered towns
  Away . . . upon the Downs.

I saw green banks of daffodil,
  Slim poplars in the breeze,
Great tan-brown hares in gusty March
  A-courting on the leas,
And meadows with their glittering streams and silver scurrying dace :
  Home—what a perfect place !

If there is little or no shadow of the war over the pages of either of these poets it is either because their poems were written before the war darkened over us or, as with Colwyn Philipps, like the soldier poets of old, they preferred to forget it awhile in their verses and remember, instead, the happier things they had known before it and hoped to know again after. Colwyn Philipps was the eldest son of Lord St. Davids. He had resolved to make the Army his profession while he was still at Eton; the war found him a captain in the Horse Guards; and you have only to read the poems and letters in his book to see how completely he realised Chaucer's ideal of the soldier and was ' a very perfect gentle knight.' To stoop to any creed of military ' frightfulness ' would have been utterly impossible for the brotherly, high-minded man who carelessly unlocked his heart in the verses which were published after he had been killed in action near Ypres, on 13th May 1915. You may know from his poems that he loved children and dogs and horses; was a keen sportsman, fond of the open-air life; was scornful of social and religious humbug and hypocrisy; was quick to sympathise with the underdog and indignant with those who oppressed the poor. Withal, he had a delightful sense of humour, and it plays freely through the letters from the front in which he makes light of discomforts and danger and is charmed by the kindness of his French hosts and the affection that springs up betwixt him and their children; and a letter from a Horse Guards trooper tells you with what ardour and heroism he went at last to his death at the head of his men.

Here is what you learn of his personality from his poems. Not only in 'Half Time' does he pull up to look into the heart of things and give them their real value :

> Warrior, cease your fight awhile,
> Look upon the heap of spoil.
> Are these things so greatly blessed
> That you ever upward pile ?
> Always onward you have pressed,
> But you soon must seek your rest.
> *Are* these things worth while ?

As for what he feels to be worth while—

> I love thee as I love the holiest things,
> Like perfect poetry and angels' wings,
> And cleanliness and sacred motherhood,
> And all things simple, sweetly pure, and good.
> I love thee as I love a little child. . . .

Or again, from ' Attainment ' :

> When you have grasped the highest rung,
> When the last hymn of praise is sung,
> When all around you thousands bow,
> When Fame with laurel binds your brow,
> When you have reached the utmost goal
> That you have set your hurrying soul. . . .
> Then you shall see the whole thing small
> Beside the one gift worth it all :
> The one good thing from pole to pole
> Is called Simplicity of Soul.

All which is of a piece with the poem to his mother:

> Can I make my feeble art
> Show the burning of my heart? . . .
> Every day and every hour
> I have battened on your power,
> While you taught of life the whole;
> You my best beloved and nighest,
> You who ever claimed the highest
> Was the one and only goal. . . .
> When the sands of life seemed sliding
> You were helping, you were guiding—
> Claimed for me the glorious rôle:
> You my loved one and no other,
> You my only lovely Mother,
> You the pilot of my soul;

and it is of a piece with that last letter he wrote to his mother before her death in March 1915: 'This is not a letter, it's a testimonial. I give you a character of twenty-six years. You have never advised me to do anything because it seemed wise unless it was the highest right. Single-minded you have chosen love and honour as the " things that are more excellent," and you have not failed. . . . You are to me the dearest friend, the perfect companion, the shining example, and the proof that honour and love are above all things and are possible of attainment.' Pessimists and the few self-righteous who make a virtue of shirking their duty in this crisis that has threatened to overwhelm us as a nation have sneered and cast superior doubts upon the sincerity of the ideals for which the best sons of Britain have unselfishly sacrificed all that was theirs to offer, but their fussy complacency and narrow love of self shrink to their true proportions beside the moral and spiritual stature of such a man as Colwyn Philipps. And he was no exception, but stood, as you shall see, for the same human ideals that made fighting-men of all these soldier poets, and of the many thousands like them in heart and mind who have had no gift of song.

Nicholas Todd was another lover of

children. Born at Occold, Suffolk, in 1878, he was educated at Felsted and Keble College, then became in succession assistant master at Balham, and from 1906 to 1916, at Sedbergh School. He wrote charmingly whimsical plays, with the liveliest songs scattered through them, for his boys to act, and two of these, 'The Sacred Lobster' and 'The Bridge of Rainbows,' are printed at the end of a memorial volume. One who knew him says he seemed to bear 'a mysterious passport to the intimacy of children'; and that 'it was scarcely conceivable that he could ever have done other than teach boys to call the wild flowers by their names, to write painful Latin elegies, to love the becks and the fells, bird and beast, the satire of Gilbert and Sullivan, the human sympathy of Dickens. For all this was something more to him than a profession, a thing to be laid aside in leisure hours '—and in his leisure he wrote those plays and songs for his boys' amusement. His humour and love of nature and of children and of all life overflows his poems, and only once or twice does any hint of the war get into them. In August 1915 he recalls two friends who used to walk the heather with him, and now :

> One is far away where the heroes stand
> For the right of God and the motherland.
>
> Another waits where the spire looks down
> On the level plains round the Saxon town.
>
> They have the gleam of the light divine,
> The loss and the loneliness are mine.

In a different vein, just after he had joined the Queen's Westminsters as a private, he wrote a rhyming epistle from Hazely Down Camp, Winchester, on Easter Eve, 1916 :

> Dear Meg, now I 'm a simple Tommy
> I thought you would like a letter from me,
> Living a silent celibut
> With twenty others in a hut,
> My bed of wooden boards and tressels
> And blankets thick with which one wrestles,

While the cold night wind through the door
Keeps time to rats that scour the floor;
A sergeant stern with language rude
Who tells me that my drilling's crude,
And boots two inches thick which they
Make me to clean three times a day. . . .

Who would have thought that I should go
To fight against a foreign foe?
If I return with half a leg
You'll run much faster than me, Meg,
And in a race around the yard
You'll beat me hollow, which is hard.
I shall forget in forming fours,
And other motions used by corps,
That ever I took interest
In dulce et decorum est.

And so—farewell if when May comes,
And snow-white gleam the garden plums,
You run across the yard to school,
Hair-braided, with your reticule,
Then think of me, my little maid,
Forming for nine o'clock parade,
And making an egregious hash
Of drill, and growing a moustache!
This thought, that the same evening star
Shines on us both, though severed far,
And guides us on our unknown way,
Should cheer us all from day to day.

This 'gentle and vivacious little figure,' after six months of soldiering, was killed in France in October 1916, and when you have grown intimate with him in his verse you will feel it is the veriest truth of him that shines in the lines written on his death by an anonymous friend who fancies him arriving earth-dusty in Paradise with quick, impulsive stride and a deprecating, rather derisive smile for any acclamations that greet him when the word is passed :

. . . This man knew joy and grief; was wise
Where others stumbled, loved the fragrant earth
And flowers and winds and quiet autumnal skies ;
He gave men laughter, nursed the frailest birth
Of fancy—joyed in comradeship ; his mind
Was quick in mystery, pondered in the shade,
Loathed war and cruelty—was unafraid.

And as the whisper passed, the dreaming ways,
Perchance, awoke as magic ; all your days
Came hurrying with phantom feet to bind
A wreath of flowers on your reluctant head.
I like to think, how you who loved not praise,
Endured the welcome of the clear-eyed dead.

Photo by E. O. Hoppé.

EDWARD THOMAS.
LIEUT., ROYAL GARRISON ARTILLERY.

He loved Sedbergh, and Sedbergh loved him, and you may be sure there will not be lacking some who will henceforth see him return to it as he saw other shadows return in such nights as he commemorates in ' The Old Schoolroom ' :

In the silence of the school-room, among the desks deserted,
Ink-stained and marred by marks of many hands,
Through the windows in the moonlight by driving rain-clouds skirted,
Come the visions of Old Boys from many lands.
And quietly and mournfully they take their well-known places,
And their books lie open by them on the form,
And they see, as in a mist-wraith, the old forgotten faces
With the scar-marks of the world's eternal storm.

Whilst Nicholas Todd was teaching at Sedbergh School, Robert Sterling was one of the students there. In 1912, Sterling went from Sedbergh to Pembroke College, Oxford. He was a brilliant classical scholar, fond enough of boating and football, but his love of literature, especially of poetry, dwarfed most of his other interests. 'He was something of a visionary,' says the friend who writes the memoir in his book; ' he used to wish that he could draw, feeling that so only—by artistic as well as literary expression, as in Blake—could he give adequate expression to his ideas. A serenity, and at times a certain dreamy wistfulness were peculiarly typical of him, and the quiet strength that comes of a firm hold upon a principle of life.' He had a genius for friendship, but ' never courted friendships; his friends grew around him, and they learnt that the force which had drawn them to him became stronger with closer contact. . . . His friendship ennobled, because his nature was less mundane, more spiritual than that of the ordinary mortal. He went about life in the same manner as did the knight-errant of old, who would give his purse to the first wandering beggar he met and forget all about it in a moment.

Material things were taken as they came ;
if they did not come he wasted little time
in trying to get them.'

The spirit and fascination of Oxford
took a wonderful hold upon his heart and
imagination, as you may gather from the
six poems he has dedicated to her praise.
See with what magic he pictures her in
' Oxford—First Vision,' and the aspirations
that vision wakens in him :

I saw her bowed by Time's relentless hand,
Calm as cut marble, cold and beautiful,
As if old sighs through the dim night of years,
Like frosted snowflakes on the silent land,
Had fallen : and old laughter and old tears,
Old tenderness, old passion, spent and dead,
Had moulded her their stony monument :
   While ghostly memory lent
Treasure of form and harmony to drape her head. . . .

Oh, could I pluck (methought) from out yon breast
A share of her rich mystery, and feel,
Flushing my soul with new adventurous zeal
The fiery perfume of that flame-born flower,
Which grows in man to God : then I might wrest
Glad secrets from the past—the golden dower
Of the world's sunrise and young glimmering East.

And the same feeling stirring the same longings is in the sonnet to Oxford:

> . . . Trees draw their sacrifice of greenery
> From the old charnels that repose beneath;
> So let me feel the impulse of thy breath,
> Like an enchanter's spell, awakening me
> To thy new treasures of Eternity
> Bursting from out the pregnant soils of Death. . . .

But two years saw the end of these dreams, when the war brought his Oxford career to a close. He won the Newdigate Prize of 1914 with his poem, 'The Burial of Sophocles'; and in the August of that year, just after war was declared, he obtained a commission in the Royal Scots Fusiliers. By the following February he was out in France, and was killed on the evening of St. George's Day, 1916, after holding his trench all day against the enemy's onslaughts.

All the war verse in his book consists of two quatrains—one in memory of a friend, and one which may be taken as a response to Germany's famous or infamous Hymn:

> Ah, hate like this would freeze our human tears,
>   And stab the morning star:
> Not it, not it commands and mourns and bears
>   The storm and bitter glory of red war.

Few of our soldier poets who have gone wrote verse so mature in thought and finished in style as Robert Sterling's.

> It might not seem a youth's imaginings,
> But to an Attic age might well belong,

says Roger Quin, in his beautiful memorial sonnet; and there is one stanza of Sterling's 'Burial of Sophocles' that lingers with me as his own fitting epitaph:

> Ah, surely there is wonder and strange stir
> Amid Earth's guardian gods, when the last goal
> Hath gained the crown, and to Earth's sepulchre
> We bear the way-worn chariot of the soul!
> And surely here a memory shall last,
> In hill and grove and torrent, of this day,
> For bards to glean who can: and they shall sing
>   How the sweet singer passed
> Forth to his rest with war about his way
> And a dread mask of Ares menacing!

So far as I can learn, Scott Craven wrote nothing—at all events he printed nothing—after he doffed his civilian habit and became a captain in the Buffs. His 'Joe Skinner,' which was published over eleven years ago, before he had made a reputation as an actor, is the tale of a man,

> So good and kind-hearted, so meek and so mild,
> With the face of a satyr, the heart of a child,

who died broken and in poverty, a pariah, and misjudged by reason of the sinister sneer, belying his character, that was stamped on his face from birth—a tale in the Ingoldsby manner, told with much of Barham's irresponsible humour and rhyming and metrical cleverness, with passages of tenderness and odd pathos such as Barham seldom attempted. The ideas, sentiments, aspirations that run through the miscellaneous poems he wrote in the years before the war are in complete harmony with the spirit in which he promptly took up arms when the war came.

'The Cross in the Rock,' with its insistence that 'Love and Right shall rule for aye,' might almost have been written in anticipation of the ordeal we are now enduring :

> Though Justice for a while delay
> When the oppressed to her hath cried,
> No righteous tear is shed in vain,
> And Time no wrong hath justified.
> For every jot unjustly ta'en
> A tyrant nation yet shall pay,
> And deep the cup of penance drain.

He unfolds his faith in 'Life's Prologue,' that whatever poor part may be given to us, and however cramped and sorry the setting, we should scorn to have any doubt or fear but 'hold the stage like men'; and reiterates it in 'The Song of the Stars' :

> . . . Then like grim warriors of old
>   Let's glory in our scars,
> And read aright, my doubting wight,
>   God's emblem of the stars :
> Our highest, best achieved—behold,
>   A higher niche and sphere !

> Nor deem the battle lost or won,
> There's something yet beyond the sun
> When our brief thread of life is spun
> > And sorrows disappear :
> A myriad suns beyond the sun,
> > Serene, resplendent, clear !

He wrote a play of Hereward the Wake, *The Last of the English*, that has real poetic and dramatic qualities ; and a little before the war he was telling me, in his eager, sanguine fashion, of another play he meant to write, a romance of modern life that should get away from the squalor of the realists and preach a more idealistic philosophy—but all that ended when he fell gallantly in April 1917 heading his men in an attack on the German lines.

Nothing of the war enters into the poems of Harold Parry, though many of them were written whilst he was on active service and sent home on odd scraps of paper. He was just turned twenty when he was killed by a shell in Flanders on

6th May 1917. The romance of war had no lure for him, but it is easy to understand how impossible it was for one who held, as he so obviously did, by the old sanctities and ideals of progress and human right to stand apart and see them desecrated and destroyed under the iron heel of the Hun. There is the true gold of poetry and promise that can never be fulfilled in the best of his work—in 'A Song of Youth,' the 'Ode to Death,' some of the love songs, and in the 'Ode to Dusk,' with its exquisite close—

> Listen. I hear the trumpets of the angels wind
> Their call across the bordered infinite;
> And Dusk with all her panoply of falling light,
> Is gone to kneel, adoring, at the feet
> Which Mary Magdalen anointed, meet,
> With richest spikenard
> And fragrant costliest nard.

His sympathies went out to the weak and the wronged; for all his youth, he had probed much into the world's unhappiness and was passionate to help to bring in the reign of justice and righteousness, and ' with a practical, old-fashioned piety sought to obey the commandment, Thou shalt love thy neighbour as thyself.' He, too, had a great love for children and felt that

> The simplest things in life are loveliest:
> The smile of little children whose sweet eyes
> Have not yet ceased from wistful wondering,
> And innocent, as though the melodies
> Of Life were all they knew—and cleanly things
> Were all they saw and all they cared to see.

He had made history and political science his special studies, and won the Queen's Prize for History at his school and an Open History Scholarship at Oxford. Swinburne, Wordsworth, Keats, and Francis Thompson were his favourite poets, and a copy of A. E. Housman's 'A Shropshire Lad' was found on his dead body.

' I am going to try to get into the Army at the end of this term, I think,' he wrote to his mother from Oxford, three weeks before his nineteenth birthday. 'I have no wish to remain a civilian any longer; and, though the whole idea of war is against my conscience, I feel that in a time of national crisis like the present the individual has no right whatever to urge his views if they are contrary to the best and immediate interest of the State.'

Less than a year later, a lieutenant in the King's Royal Rifles, he is writing to his sister from France: 'In general, the whole of the war zone is so un-Christian in its aspect and so horrible in its antithesis to all that is beautiful and good that I would rather not write about it. I do my best to forget and, in a measure, to forgive it by reading Keats, Blake, Swinburne or Housman, and even by attempts to write poems on the *things* of life, not the sins of it.' He goes on to say that he believes man is now being made to pay for the sins of his body with his body; that for centuries civilisation has been on the wrong track; 'man has developed his physical mind almost to the utter exclusion of his spiritual self'; that all manner of new inventions have been designed to increase his bodily comfort; he has given himself up to the worship of gold, values it for its own sake and the luxury it can give him. He would have little hope of raising the world out of this slough, ' but there are the children,' he says, ' and if only we can develop them along the new or, rather, the old right lines we shall have done something. The mind of a child is a most beautiful thing. I have told you—have I not, Kiddie?—that I am passionately fond of children, though I think that no one at home realises how strong that passion is, and I have never told any one yet what I had determined long ago to do after I left Oxford. To-day, when there is a possibility of death to be faced, I can tell you all. I had decided, no matter how successful I was at Oxford, to go and teach at an ordinary secondary school—best of all at the old, old school itself—for there I should meet the material upon which I could work. I want to teach children what love and beauty are, and how infinitely better goodness is than mere satisfaction—is it satisfaction?—of physical desires.' A high and wonderful ambition in one so young, and wonderfully significant that this boy could cherish it hopefully still amid scenes of savage slaughter and devastation where, as he was presently writing to his mother, everything was 'absolutely inhuman and unlovely : all that relieves the sordidness of the business is the pluck and cheeriness of the boys, and that is amazing to a degree.' He is so possessed by that ambition of his that it comes into several of his letters. To his friend Mundy, touching on his love of children and his longing to be of service to them, he writes, ' I have never attempted to analyse why exactly this love is so strong, though probably it is because children are so pure and innocent and unstained as much as may be by the sins of civilisation. This is the material upon which we must begin our gigantic task. Let us show to the child that there are greater and more wonderful things in the world than self and money; let us see that the instinctive love of beauty and the right things, which is such a wonderful prerogative of children, is fostered and developed by every means in our power, and when these children grow up they, much more than we, will be able to further this great revolution of the state of man. . . . Mundy, I feel sure that this is no idle dream—it is too beautiful for that; beautiful because its prospect satisfies as no dream ever can.'

As for the pacifists who cry that our one aim should be to make peace as quickly as possible on the best terms we can get, he sees too clearly to wish for that and writes under the hourly menace of death, ' Though war is so inhuman, especially in its utter severance of man from everything for which he cares, it is infinitely preferable to peace while yet the devil has not been cast out of Germany.' And again, ' One thing is certain—we must never, never lay up for our children a heritage such as has been bequeathed to us. It is not right, it is not fair, it is vastly inhuman and too devilish to be anything but evil to the core. . . . Peace now means many things. It means first and foremost and very personally the saving of many, many lives. It means that the boys who have gone to war with laughter in their eyes and God in their heart can return to the ways they knew and loved so well. It means that perhaps many of them—perhaps even I—may one day make my way back to home and security and comfort. But, on the other hand, it means this—that the great sacrifice we have already made, the sacrifice of a million young lives is wasted. If we made peace now—peace on the basis our enemies suggest—we should find our hands, our hearts and, yea, our very souls touched with blood-guiltiness. We should have saved our own lives at the expense of all those who have died and all those dear and beautiful and lovely children as yet hidden deep in the vales of the future. For these we should have left a heritage like unto which our sorrow of to-day would be as joy. Let us put aside our personal feeling in this matter—though God knows it is deep and bitter enough—and by making our sacrifice perfect ensure the future happiness of the world. It is our happiness, or the happiness of countless thousands in the years when we, in any case, shall be no more.'

Some of the best of Henry Lionel Field's poems, such as the charming lyric ' Plough-

HUGH REGINALD FRESTON (REX).
LIEUT., ROYAL BERKSHIRE REGT.

man, Dig the Coulter Deep,' were written in his Oxford days. He was the favourite grandson of Mr. Jesse Collings and traced his descent, on the distaff side, from Cromwell. From Marlborough he went to Oxford, and matriculated for Lincoln College, but instead of going there preferred to start at once on what he meant to be the real work of his life, and became a student at the Birmingham School of Art. In July 1914, he was taking holiday at a sketching school at Coniston, when the sudden outbreak of war brought him hurrying home to enlist. He was persuaded to wait for a commission, and in due course was gazetted to the Royal Warwickshire Regiment, and in February 1916 was sent to France with his men. For five months he was in the trenches, and wrote home saying he was enjoying himself. 'I am much happier than I ever thought I should be in the Army. After all, I am in my destined place, and doing or about to do what I should be doing or about to do. In some way or another, home seems nearer, and thank God I don't flinch from the sound of the guns.' On another occasion, he wrote about himself and his brother, who was also in the firing line, ' It is our birthright to do something of this sort once in our lives. I honestly don't wish things otherwise, neither does Guy. I don't mean to talk about Spartan mothers, and that sort of thing. . . . But remember we are all part of each other, and think of it like this—when we leave you, it is not so much you losing us as you fighting through the medium of your sons.' He was killed in the Great Push of 1st July 1916; he had led his men forward and they had swept after him triumphantly over the first and second German trenches; he had called a laughing remark to a brother officer and was raising his hand as the signal for a further advance when a bullet struck him down. The trail of the war is over the drawings reproduced from his pocket sketch-book and over half a dozen of his twenty-six poems. He put his love of home into the lines addressed to ' J. C. F.' less than two months before he fought his last fight :

Sweet are the plains of France where the Lent lilies blow,
Yet sweeter far the woods and fields I know.
Fair is the land where the lark sings at dawn,
Yet fairer far the land where I was born.

No nightingale can sing a lovelier lay
Than that the sparrows chirp in my roof tree,
French suns can never paint a brighter day
Than that my fog-bound coasts can offer me.

But it is a sense of the tragedy and waste of it all that moves him in the rest of his war verse, as in the unfinished ' Carol for Christmas, 1914 ' :

> On a dark midnight such as this
>   Nearly two thousand years ago,
> Three kings looked out towards the East
>   Where a single star shone low. . . .

> Be with them, Lord, in camp and field
> >   Who guard our ancient name to-night.
> Hark to the cry that rises now,
> >   Lord, Lord, maintain us in our right.
>
> Be with the dying, be with the dead,
> >   Sore stricken far on alien ground,
> Be with the ships on clashing seas
> >   That gird our island kingdom round.
>
> Through barren nights and fruitless days
> >   Of wasting, when our faith grows dim,
> Mary, be with the stricken heart,
> >   Thou hast a Son, remember Him. . . .

and in a broken verse at the end he prays that the purpose of all the welter of death into which he is going may be made clear to him.

Racing, polo, the joys of the chase were the main themes of the ringing, virile songs that Captain George Robins wrote before he turned his back on sport and went on the great adventure into France, where he died in action on 5th May 1915. All the company he commanded on Hill 60 were killed, except his orderly, when, fatally gassed, he contrived to crawl down and make his report with his dying breath. Educated at Haileybury and at Magdalen, Captain Robins left Oxford to obtain a commission in the East Yorkshire Regiment during the Boer War, and in 1901 went on service to South Africa, attached to the Mounted Infantry. He resigned from his regiment a year after it returned to England, and became partner in a firm of London and China merchants. Marrying in 1905, he and his wife went to Shanghai, where he remained for two years on his firm's business. He was in Shanghai again when Germany invaded Belgium. 'As he was in sole charge of the business out there,' writes his brother, in a biographical note to George Robins' *Lays of the Hertfordshire Hunt*, 'it was not until December that he was able to fulfil the one wish of his heart and come home at once to offer his services to his country. Between August and December 1914 he was terribly impatient at his enforced exile. Writing of the battle of the Aisne he said: " I know of one gentleman of England . . . who thinks himself accurs'd he was not there." I think he was never so pleased to see any one in his life as he was to welcome the man who came out to take his place and so set him free to come home. My brother was an idealist, and to him his King and Country were not mere names, but a very real part of himself. That he came from the other end of the world to fight for them is, I think, sufficient proof of the realness of his feelings.' In February 1915 he rejoined his old regiment, as captain of the 3rd Battalion, and in France, in April, was transferred to the 2nd Battalion of the Duke of Wellington's Regiment, which he was commanding in his last fight. At home, in happier years, he was assistant secretary of the Hertfordshire Hunt, and the keenest of sportsmen. He was fond of poetry, but sport came first, and inspires most of the best of his verse. Yet his 'Best of All' was not sport, and it is to her he turns in 'L'Envoi':

> . . . War is good when the stress is past
>   And the rankling scars grow old,
> For its rigours fade and its glamours last
>   Till the sombre grey turns gold;
> And the hunger and thirst and the bitter days
>   No more in our thoughts find place,
> But we mind that we trod life's roughest ways,
>   And met death face to face;
> And the soul's astir and the brain's afire
>   For the good fight fought before,
> But the heart knows well there is something higher
>   Than the clamorous ways of war.
> Faint on the ear grows the bugle call,
> And we turn once more to the Best of All. . . .

The most charming of love songs are his two called 'Roses,' one from Pretoria, and one from Shanghai; and the spirit of his loyal comradeship glows in his lines, 'To the Others':

. . . Rhymes are halting and verses weak,
Thoughts ring truer than words can speak.
Proudly I fill the wine-glass up
And I pledge you all in a loving cup.
Here's to the cheery days gone by
When we marched in the ranks of the old M.I.
And still in the future, come what may,
Be it sport or war, be it work or play,
I ask no better than just to ride
Shoulder to shoulder, side by side,
With the men whose mettle I've proved and tried,
    Comrades of mine.

This was written when he was leaving the Army after the Boer War, and 'the others' were five of the officers who had been through the South African campaign with him. Three of the five have now died, as he has, in this war. At the end of his book is a list of fourteen of his friends, followers of the Hertfordshire Hunt, who have also gallantly followed him to death in France.

CHARLES J. B. MASEFIELD, M.C.
LIEUT. (ACTING-CAPT.), 5TH NORTH STAFFS. REGT.

Bernard White

With one or two exceptions Bernard Charles de Boismaison White's poems date from before the war. Born at Harlesden in 1886, on his father's side, says a memoir by de V. Payne-Payne, he was connected with the French family of de Boismaison, his grandmother having been the daughter of Bernard de Boismaison (son of Louis XVI.'s ophthalmic surgeon) who came to England at the Revolution and settled at Chichester, where his son taught dancing. After a year's apprenticeship to a London printer, Bernard White obtained a post, in 1910, in the publishing house of Messrs. Hutchinson, and thence went, in 1912, into the publicity department of the Marconi Company, and was presently acting also as assistant editor of the *Wireless World*. 'Nothing was further from his thoughts than a soldier's life,' but in September 1914, when Germany was entrenched within a day's march of Paris and there was dire need of men for our

Army, he joined the Officers' Training Corps of the London University. The following February he was gazetted to the York and Lancaster Regiment, but in June was persuaded to transfer to the Tyneside Scottish (20th Northumberland Fusiliers), and went to France with that regiment on the 1st January 1916. ' War is the most horrible, inconceivable, inhuman sacrifice it is possible to imagine,' he wrote to his brother in February. . . . ' I am with you, and very close, too ; for after all, am I not fighting for the little home in peaceful England that is at present so sad ? '

His only poems of the war are a translation into verse of the speech delivered by M. Henri Lavisse at the Sorbonne in December 1914—a quaint Struwwelpeter parody :

> Let us see if William can
> Make war like a gentleman. . . .

and ' Pro Patria,' to the Empire's Service

of Wireless Operators with whom he had been associated in his peace-time business:

   . . . Ye in our camps, our ships, the stations that
      gird our seas,
Holding in trust the key and power of the sacred
      flame
For England's greater honour, let not your service
      cease
Till ye confirm your royal right to the scroll of Fame,
          Till on the key
          Of Victory
For the troubled ears of the world ye tap out the
      signal—Peace.

' One of his outstanding qualities was his love of children,' writes the editor of his book, and you might guess as much from the simple and charming poem ' To Guy.'

Until he joined the Artists' Rifles in 1915, when he was thirty-seven and might have been excused if he had not volunteered, Edward Thomas had written all his poetry in prose. There is a delicate play of fancy and imagination and a lapidary cunning in the verbal artistry of his essays and criticisms which make it less surprising that he should at last have found a medium of expression in verse than that he did not find it earlier. But none even of his intimates can have foreseen that, with his gentle manners, his diffident self-distrust and bookish preoccupations, he had in him the makings of a soldier. Chivalry, the finest sense of honour, steadiness of purpose and a quiet courage we always knew that he had; what took us by surprise was the completeness with which he threw aside his civilian habit of pleasant bohemianism, subdued himself to military discipline and grew cheerfully hardened to the rougher life of camp and training ground. Certainly, he was no lover of war; he answered the call to arms solely because he had a conscience and felt it was his duty to do so; then, with his usual thoroughness, he was not satisfied to make a pretence of being what he had set out to become. He devoted himself as keenly and as scrupulously to his military work as he had done to the literary work that was more properly his. He was impatient of the prolonged training and was not contented till he secured a commission in the Royal Garrison Artillery and was sent to France.

It was this compelling impulse, since he was a soldier, to be the real thing and share in the worst that befell his comrades, that took him to his death during the British advance in April 1917. 'For,' says his friend John Freeman, ' in France he was detached from his battery for staff duties, and was dissatisfied until he had succeeded in returning to his old post of danger. Just the same scrupulous spirit had moved him years before when he gave up a permanent appointment sans duties, because there was no way in which he could earn or was expected to earn his pay. There were things he could not endure; no one who knew him could be surprised.' He volunteered for the dangerous work of serving on an observation post, and was killed by a shell.

All his poems were written in the atmosphere of war, during his training days or while he was at the front, but apart from a rousing call in ' The Trumpet '—

> Open your eyes to the air
> That has washed the eyes of the stars
> Through all the dewy night :
> Up with the light,
> To the old wars ;
> Arise, arise !—

the ' In Memoriam ' quatrain for Easter 1915—

The flowers left thick at nightfall in the wood
This Eastertide call into mind the men,
Now far from home, who, with their sweethearts, should
Have gathered them, and will do never again—

and apart from a stray line or so glooming in some picture of country life, like a cloud that drifts momentarily across the sun, there is little of the influence of war in them—less than there is in the songs of Francis Ledwidge. Both were lovers of nature and poured their love of her into verse of an exquisite simplicity, but Thomas was the more reticent, the more scholarly; he had not Ledwidge's artlessness, and though he had the same emotional tenderness was not so simply unreserved in revealing it. The war stirred both of them profoundly and absorbed their energies, but whenever they had leisure to withdraw into themselves, for them, as for others of their temper, old sources of inspiration reopened, old habits of thought closed round them again, and in such hours of respite they returned to the familiar inner life from which they had been exiled, and the war dwindled to nothing but a weeping of rain on the window, a wind that wailed in the darkness and rattled at the door which shut it out.

Photo by J. Soame, Oxford.

EWART ALAN MACKINTOSH, M.C.
LIEUT., SEAFORTH HIGHLANDERS.

IV

Humbly, O England, we offer what is of little worth,
Just our bodies and souls and everything else we have;
But thou with thy holy cause wilt hallow our common earth,
Giving us strength in the battle—and peace, if need, in the grave.

    Acting-Captain Charles J. B. Masefield, M.C.—
    Enlisted, or The Recruits.

WHAT finally emerges from the songs of all these dead singers is a gracious but unconquerable spirit of humanity—a sane, civilised spirit, common to them all, that hated war with a hatred that was only strengthened and intensified by contact with the horrors and primeval barbarities of it. The burden of their singing is always that they fight, not for fighting's sake, but to break the last stronghold of ancient savagery, to enthrone Right above Might, to blaze a trail through the dark forest by which the men of to-morrow may find their way into a new and happier world where war shall be no more. From the heights of their idealism this was the hope, the promised land that they could see. They did not expect to reach it themselves; theirs was only that far-off Pisgah-view of it; but they were touched with pride in the thought that they were privileged to give their lives that through them it might remain an inheritance for the generations yet to come. This was all that mattered, and for themselves—

> My day was happy—and perchance
> The coming night is full of stars,

writes Richard Dennys, in one of his *Ballads of Belgium,* and in another,

> Death flies by night, Death flies by day,
>   He calls the gay, he calls the sad,
> And if he summon me away,
>   Be sure my going will be glad.

Life had not offered an easy road to Major John E. Stewart; from his boyhood he had fought bravely against poverty and circumstance and won by hard work every honour that came to him. He proved his capacity at school, took his M.A. degree at Glasgow University, and settled down as a teacher at Langloan Public School, Coatbridge. But within a month of the declaration of war he saw his duty clear, threw everything aside and joined the Highland Light Infantry as a private. He received a commission after two months' service, and was attached to a Border Regiment, in which he rose to be captain and adjutant. Presently, with the rank of major, he was transferred to the South Lancashire Regiment. By then he had seen much fighting in France, and had been given the command of a battalion of the Staffordshire Regiment when he met his death in action on the 26th February 1918. Two years before that he had won the Military Cross for conspicuous bravery in the field. He had written a good deal of prose and verse in peace-time for many periodicals, and from more than one poem in *Grapes of Thorns*, the book of verse he published in 1917, you may know in what mind he went to his death—

> If I should fall upon the field
>   And lie among the slain,
> Then mine will be the victory
>   And yours the pain ;
> For this in prospect comforts me
>   Against all saddening fears
> That, dying so, I make myself
>   Worthy your tears.

He puts into 'The Messines Road' that burning sympathy for France and resolve to right the wrongs she is enduring which have fired so many of our men who have fallen in her defence, and none has paid her higher or more splendid tribute than he laid at the feet of her heroes in his song of 'Verdun.' There is a striking 'Ode of the Poet' in which he speaks of how, amid the hell of modern battle, the bard of these days laughs at Homer and the sheltered muse of Tennyson, and foresees that a new poet shall yet arise to sing the new Iliad, that he may be with us unknown at this hour, enduring all the agonies and horrors of war that shall live for ever in the song he shall make when, in some future quietness, he can look back and remember.

Or haply in the silent womb of Time
Stirs the elected spirit to this hour,
He who will build for us the lofty rhyme,
Wearing a god-like vision as his dower,
Wise in the things that he has learned in Heav'n,
And wiser even than he who here has striven
For that he sees as the holy angels see
The foolishness we deem felicity,
And all the dreadful things beneath the sun
Which we have made to grieve the holy One.
He with His scales
Shall justly weigh us out our due,
And winnow with His righteous flails
The chaff from out the crop we grew.
But this is sure, howe'er it be,
We shall not face ashamedly
The reckoning. For all the price
Of our poor faults is doubly paid
In valour and in sacrifice.
Who, then, of judgment is afraid?

Loathing war, yet seeing no honourable way of avoiding it, he faced the worst manfully, fearing no enemy and afraid only lest he should show fear when death seemed imminent and give those he loved cause to be ashamed of him, but—

> Lo, when I joined the fight,
>   And bared my breast
> To all the darts of that wild, hellish night,
>   I only stood the test,
> For Fear, which I had feared, deserted then,
>   And forward blithely to the foe I prest,
> King of myself again.
>
> Blessed be God above
>   For His sweet care,
> Who heard the prayers of those whom most I love
>   And my poor suppliance there,
> Who brought me forth in life and limb all whole,
>   Who blessed my powers with His divine repair,
> And gave me back my soul!

A far other war-song this, far nobler in its humility and more courageous than the brazen, sounding rhymes that our civilian war-poets used to sing for us!

It was nothing strange that these men, nurtured in peace, reared wholly in the gentler arts of life, should enter so suddenly into the new and abhorrent atmosphere of war, haunted, more or less, by premonitions that they would never return. This premonition recurs in the verse of most of them and is accepted sometimes stoically and as a matter of course, sometimes with regret or with bitterness, but firmly and without dread, and sometimes in an eager and lofty spirit of self-sacrifice. Something of this sense of doom is in Geoffrey Bache Smith's later poems, but it leaves him untroubled, and when he hints at it it is with a calm, serene philosophy. He gave evidence of literary ability while he was still a student at King Edward's School, Birmingham. In 1912 he was elected to a History Exhibition at Corpus

Christi College, Oxford, and took up residence there in October of that year. He was looking forward to devoting himself to literature as a profession when the war, at a stroke, shattered all his plans, and he at once joined the Oxford O.T.C. In January 1916 he obtained a commission in the Oxford and Bucks Regiment, but was transferred to the 19th Lancashire Fusiliers and went with them to France in November 1915. He had a hard winter in the trenches and was in the thick of the fighting in July 1916. His letters home show how profoundly he was impressed by the horrors of war, but his native cheerfulness never failed him; his humour and good spirits were proof against all the darkness and danger of his surroundings. After the Somme advance he was made intelligence officer, and then adjutant. While walking down a village street on 29th November 1916, he was struck by a fragment of a stray shell; the wound seemed slight but became septic, and he died three days later. Shortly afterwards his brother was killed in Mesopotamia, and they were the only sons of their mother, who was a widow.

His earlier poems are filled with the sweetness of common life, or the dreams and glamour of old romance, the longest and one of the best of them, 'Glastonbury,' steeped in the light and atmosphere of far-off days, being an Arthurian legend of the repentance of Lancelot. In 'A Preface for a Tale I never Told' he says that in it there shall be

> No song
> That men shall sing in battle and remember
> When they are old and grey, beside the fire :
> Only a story gathered from the hills,
> And the wind crying of forgotten days. . . .

Of the beauty and the happiness of the 'old quiet things' of life all his poetry was fashioned till the war broke through his dreams and, with 'We who have Bowed

Ourselves to Time,' he bade farewell to them:

> . . . We who have led, by gradual ways,
> Our placid life to sterner days,
>   And for old quiet things
>   Have set the strife of kings,
>
> Who battled have with bloody hands
> Through evil times in barren lands,
>   To whom the voice of guns
>   Speaks but no longer stuns,
>
> Calm, though with death encompassed,
> That watch the hours go overhead,
>   Knowing too well we must
>   With all men come to dust. . . .

And in 'Anglia Valida in Senectute' glimmers a knowledge that not only the beauty and happiness of the world are passing away from him:

We are old, we are old, and worn and school'd with ills,
  Maybe our road is almost done,
Maybe we are drawn near unto the hills
  Where rest is and the setting sun.

He cannot, in the trenches, remember Oxford but the thought intrudes:

> A little while, and we are gone;
>   God knows if it be ours to see
> Again the earliest hoar-frost white
>   On the long lawns of Trinity.

Counting over his comrades who have fallen, he wonders:

How far now to the last of battles?
  (Listen the guns are loud to-night!)

Whatever comes, I will strike once surely,
  Once because of an ancient tryst,
Once for love of your dear dead faces
  Ere I come unto you, Shapes in the mist.

His prayer is:

> O God, the God of battles,
>   To us who intercede
> Give only strength to follow
>   Until there's no more need;
> And grant us at that ending
>   Of the unkindly quest
> To come unto the quiet isles
>   Beyond Death's starry West;

and his comfort is that there are still men who, fearing nothing,

> Love home above their own hearts' blood
> And honour more than life.

In one of those letters from which I have already quoted, Harold Parry writes to his father, on 13th February 1916, 'I saw in the *Mirror* for Wednesday or Thursday a photograph of one of Mr. D——'s friends, H. R. F., an Exonian and poet of no mean ability. He paid the final price on 24th January, and England has lost another of the men who would have been a greater credit to her in life than they can be even in this most glorious death. Tell Dorothy he wrote in various of the volumes of Oxford poetry, and I should like her to get the *Mirror* to see how much F—— and Mr. D—— were of a type—both brilliant and intellectual, driven to war by a sense of duty.' The H. R. F. referred to is Hugh Reginald Freston who, like

Hugh Reginald Freston

Harold Parry, went from Oxford into the Army. When he left Dulwich College to become an undergraduate at Exeter College Freston's intention had been to fit himself for taking holy orders, but before long he relinquished this purpose, feeling irresistibly drawn to a literary career. There is high promise in the work he has done; he had a quiet confidence in his powers and great hope of his future; but as soon as the war was upon us, he allowed no personal interests to restrain him from what he conceived to be his duty. After he had trained in the O.T.C. he was made a 2nd lieutenant in the Royal Berkshire Regiment, and though he had no liking for the new life upon which he had entered, he gave himself up to it completely and enthusiastically—' doing the thing he loathed for the thing he loved.' Early in December 1915 he was in France; a few weeks later he took his place in the front lines, and after ten days of trench fighting, was killed. These lines which are among the poems collected into his posthumous volume, *The Quest of Truth*, might have been inspired by some strange fore-knowledge of the manner of death he was to die:

> Suddenly a great noise shall fill my ears,
> Like angry waters or the roar of men ;
> I shall be dizzy, faint with many fears ;
> Blindly my hands shall clutch the air—and then
> I shall be walking neath the quiet skies,
> In the familiar land of former years,
> Among familiar faces. I shall arise
> In that dear land where there are no more tears

—for it was so death came to him. He was inspecting a dug-out which had been shelled when several shells came over and one struck him and, engulphed instantly in its burst of noise and darkness, 'from that moment,' writes his commanding officer, ' he was dead, although he breathed a few times—no suffering.'

The premonition that he was destined to die for his ideals, that he was plainly called to lay down his life for his country, and the cause that was his and hers, is in other of Freston's poems, as it is in those of many of his comrades. It is in his 'Departure,' in 'When I am Dead,' in 'Two Nights '—

And I laugh to hear the bugles, but I weep to hear the bells,
For I know the bells of Oxford will ring no more for me—

It is in 'April 1915,' and again in 'October 31st, 1915,' written not long before he left England for the last time:

After I am dead,
And have become part of the soil of France,
This much remember of me :
I was a great sinner, a great lover, and life puzzled me very much.
Ah, love ! I would have died for love !
Love can do so much both rightly and wrongly.
It remembers mothers and little children,
And lots of other things.
O men unborn, I go now, my work unfinished !
I pass on the problem to you : the world will hate you : be brave !

And more movingly and with a deeper sense of conviction it speaks through 'The Gift,' where he offers himself in sacrifice without asking why, for in his heart he knows:

... There is a certain ancient city, where he once was free and young,
>(But he leaves it now for you),

Where Oxford tales are spoken, and Oxford ways are sung,
>(But he leaves them now for you),

And his heart is often weary for that dear old river shore
And he thinks a little sadly of the days that come no more
>(But he gives them up for you).

If his dust is one day lying in an unfamiliar land,
>(England, he went for you)

O England sometimes think of him, of thousands only one,
In the dawning, or the noonday, or the setting of the sun
>(As once he thought of you),

For to him, and many like him, there seemed no other way
>(England, he asked not why)

But the giving up of all things for ever and for aye,
>(England, he asked not why),

LESLIE COULSON.

SERGT., LONDON BATT. ROYAL FUSILIERS.

And so he goes unshrinking from those dearest paths
  of home,
For he knows, great-hearted England, let whatever
  fate may come,
    You will never let him die !

Leonard Niell Cook, a Rugby and Oxford boy who had newly exchanged his student's gown for khaki, writing of 'Plymouth Sound,' tells how from the greensward he looked out across the sea he was on the eve of crossing, heard the harbour gun sound at sunset, saw

> The homing traffic on the water's breast
> Fold up their tawny wings and take their rest,

and, with the stars rising above him and 'God's quietness' about him, he thought of how soon he would be yonder in 'the gloomy courts of Fear' destined to be cut down,

> Perchance to crown the pallid brow of Death.

In the 'Envoi,' addressed to his parents before he went out from Edinburgh, Hamish Mann writes :

> Be calm. I follow where my friends have gone.
>   Have nought to fear,
> I go to herald in the Glorious Dawn
>   Which breaks not here.
>
> Be brave. A myriad mothers' sons before
>   Have trod this path . . .

and he bids them to be proud in his pride and only pray that when his hour comes there may be no stain upon his honour.

This is the end of Charles Masefield's song of his ' Sailing for Flanders ' :

> We have put life away and spurn the ways of the living ;
>   We have broken with the old selves who gathered and got,
>   And are free with the freedom of men who have not ;
> We partake the heroic fervours of giving and again giving.
>
> Was it only for death we were born of our mothers ?
>   Only for Death created the dear love of our wives?
>   Only for death and in vain we endeavoured our lives ?
> Yea, life was given to be given ; march onward, my brothers.

Which matches the earlier mood in which he took up arms, as he expresses it in *Enlisted, or The Recruits*:

Humbly, O England, we offer what is of little worth,
Just our bodies and souls and everything else we have;
But thou with thy holy cause wilt hallow our common earth,
Giving us strength in the battle—and peace, if need, in the grave. . . .

And here is the same foreshadowing in Ewart Alan Mackintosh's 'Ghosts of War':

When you and I are buried
With grasses over our head,
The memory of our fights will stand
Above this bare and tortured land
We knew ere we were dead. . . .

If men with hope and happiness to lose could thus calmly abjure it all without a tremor, it is the less to be wondered at that others who have made a waste of life and are burdened with shame and remorse, like the soldier pictured in W. H. Littlejohn's dramatic lyric 'To S——, A Man who Died Bravely,' should see a way of redemption in the sacrifice of self for the saving of the world and take the road to death glad in the certainty of gaining life by losing it :

I have plucked a blowing rosebud, and I trailed it in the mire,
I have left a spirit's temple frail grey ashes of dead fire,
—I have made a saintly woman plaything of a foul desire.

And I've quit the straight clean-seeing, I've attached the label 'cad,'
And I want to go down fighting, want to die with brain blood-mad :
I could spit into their faces when they grin, 'He's not so bad ! '

Drawn-out weeks I've strained the head-rope, weary months I've longed to start
For the last and best performance, where for once I'm given the part
Of a white man—and a little nickel devil through my heart.

Church parade, the padre gave out that damnation's no man's fate,
That you just report deficient and he never notes you late;
But I'm not a man to whine for mercy passing through hell's gate.

I don't snivel of repentance when hot tears have run to flood,
For I plucked a blowing rosebud and I trailed it in the mud,
But I'd like to lave its poor soiled petals with my body's blood.

I would leave the merest speck of gold within the filth-clogged sieve,
Gold that she and God might notice there and, noticing, forgive;
I would show I knew to die although I never learned to live.

So there's just a laughing death-song in my heart as up I plod
To the trenches, where my need will be a six-foot stretch of sod
With a plain wood cross above it—leave the rest of me to God.

Littlejohn joined the Territorial branch of the Middlesex Regiment when it was inaugurated, and had become a sergeant before the war. It is likely that the man whose story he tells was one of the motley new recruits who marched in his platoon. He had risen to be company sergeant-major when he was sniped at the battle of Arras, while in the act of cheering his company in the moment of victory. Before he went to France, he had fought at Gallipoli, and several of his ballads and poems are of incidents in that campaign, but I think I like best some later verse of his in which he accepts the probability of death for himself, not ' with a laughing death-song ' but with a prayer that matches it in perfect courage, and that, in the manner of his going, would seem to have been granted :

Lord, if it be Thy will
That I enter the great shadowed valley that lies
Silent just over the hill,
Grant they may say, ' There's a comrade that dies
Waving his hand to us still.'

> Lord, if there come the end,
> Let me find space and breath all the dearest I prize
> Into thy hands to commend:
> Then let me go, with my boy's laughing eyes,
> Smiling a word to a friend.

Yet you are not to imagine that these men took life sadly or half-heartedly or were one whit the less soldierly and fearless because such dark thoughts lurked at the backs of their minds and they sat now and then to fashion them into verse. Freston's more prevailing spirit is in his stirring sonnet 'On Going into Action,' and the gladness that was behind all his acceptance of death shouts triumphantly in another sonnet, 'O Fortunati':

> Oh happy to have lived these epic days!
>   To have seen unfold, as doth a dream unfold,
>   These glorious chivalries, these deeds of gold,
> The glory of whose splendour gilds death's ways,
> As a rich sunset fills dark woods with fire
>   And blinds the traveller's eyes. Our eyes *are* blind
>   With flaming heroism, that leaves our mind
> Dumbstruck with pride. We have had our hearts'
>   desire!

Oh happy ! Generations have lived and died
  And only dreamed such things as we have seen and known !
Splendour of men, death laughed at, death defied,
  Round the great world on the winds is their tale blown ;
Whatever pass, these ever shall abide :
  In memory's Valhalla, an imperishable throne.

Leonard Cook had won his M.C. before he died, fighting gallantly. Hamish Mann has met the fate he foresaw for himself when he wrote his ' Envoi ' and told in another song of the dream that he would not rest now on some placid hillside of home, but in France within hearing of the guns. . . .

> And I shall sleep beneath that foreign soil
>   As peacefully as e'er 'neath heather flower,
> Knowing that I have answered Duty's call,
>   Knowing that I have died in England's hour

—but he met his fate heroically leading his platoon in that Arras advance in which Littlejohn fell.

Under whatever premonitions may have

Photo by Seaman, Sheffield.
JOHN WILLIAM STREETS.
SERGT, 12TH YORK AND LANCASTER REGT.

come to him, the one firm conviction Charles Masefield carried with him into the war, and that made him indifferent to what might happen to himself was that

Right is might, and we shall prevail.

Masefield was thirty-five when he died; he had done distinguished work in literature before the war, and the growing mastery of his art that is apparent in his later work sufficiently indicates that he had not yet reached the summer of his powers. Born at Cheadle, he went from a preparatory school at Southport to Repton, in Derbyshire, where his tutor was Dr. Furneaux, the present Dean of Winchester. He gained there the Aylmer prize for Divinity and the Howe prize for English verse, writing for the latter 'A Vision of Italian Painters.' Leaving school, he was articled to his father, and later became a partner in the old family firm of solicitors at Cheadle, Messrs. Blagg,

Son and Masefield. From his childhood he had divided his affections between nature and books, and in 1908 Blackwoods published a first book of his own, a novel on rather unorthodox lines called *Gilbert Hermer*. But he was drawn more to verse than to prose, and in 1911 appeared a collection of his poems, *The Seasons' Difference*, in which you make contact with a mind that is keenly susceptible to natural beauty and to what is finest in the nature of man. Just because he was conscious of the goodness that was in men and was keen to see them live up to their highest level, he lashed with an indignant scorn their weaknesses, their snobbery, follies, meannesses, in the series of modern satires, *Dislikes*, that he published in 1914, the year that was to rouse us from many of the vanities he denounced and reawaken our slumbering ideals. It is not satire, though, that burns in the last poem in the book,

'Beauty Cast Out,' but a passionate earnestness of regret that the England of those latter years should, in Jonson's phrase, have 'let the noble and the precious go' in the race for wealth and material prosperity, that in her great towns the sense of beauty and the desire of it should have been banished by the lust for power and commercial gain :

Ye have your gains—
   Your transient gains; ah, hug them to you fast,
For after all your toilings and your pains
   Shall come a day to fling them wide at last,
Yearning for Beauty, not to be for ever baulked.
   What of you then, who when the dreamers dreamed
Sang praise of Hell; who your true treasures hawked
   For coined dust, and all your days blasphemed?

For all else dies
   But what is beautiful; the eternal dark,
Wherein nor moon nor star doth ever rise,
   Bends o'er imperial Carthage, but the spark
That lit the soul of Hellas glows unquenched still.
   Fast runs the world, and soon the massy gold
Casts from her, but her hungering mind doth fill
   With all the loveliness e'er dreamed of old.

Little we know
　Of Beauty who do never face to face
Speak with her now in all the ways we go ;
　She hath, we say, the wanton's swooning grace
And luscious tempting wiles the idle fool to snare.
　So we divorce her who has been man's wife,
And hound with insults her who still would share
　And lift his struggle and exalt his life.

Suffer us not
　Longer to clutch our drifting lies unsure ;
Lady, forgive us, who so soon forgot
　The true incredible Thou—strong, eager, pure
As fits a thought God thinks throughout His endless day—
　The something always singing overhead,
The vision man takes with him far away,
　Most radiant then when all things else lie dead.

O once adored
　Dear lady we have lost, return again,
Bring us not peace nor languors, but a sword,
　Even as death, dealing thy needful pain ;
Upbraid, accuse, destroy, but make our spirit whole,
　Come as an indignation, a desire
All unawares discerned in every soul,
　And on thy ready altars light the fire.

How was it possible for a man of such spiritual insight to hesitate when the war came with its instant appeal to all of honour and chivalry that had power with us? By then he had been four years married, and was happy in his work and in the home life with his wife and little son, but he could not rest so in his own happiness. He felt that his duty was elsewhere, and nothing could dissuade him from going where it led. The death of the head of his firm delayed him, but so soon as he could get his business affairs in order, in August 1915 he obtained a commission in the 5th North Staffordshire Regiment, and after some months of training and assistant adjutant work, went to France in June 1916. An unpublished poem written in those days, 'Candle Light,' gives a delightful sketch of his life in a French billet :

Candle light is so mellow and warm
  When a man comes in all hungry and cold,
Clotted with mud or wet with the storm—
  Only of candle-light you shall be told.

Of Madame's brave, sad eagerness
And French serenity of dress,
Her quiet, quick ways as she goes
To dry our heavy, sodden clothes
And bring all hot the great ragoût
That makes once more a man of you,
Her pains to help us put away
The sights that we have seen all day,
Her talk of kine, and oats, and rye,
And François' feats when but so high—
You 'd never guess, did you not know,
He died for France three months ago.
And then there 's Marthe, whom he has left
(So proud, and yet so all bereft),
And Marie, with her hair in ties,
Looking at you with great round eyes
That make you wish to Heaven you were
The hero that you seem to her.
And last, and least,
There 's François' little Jean-Baptiste,
For whom, deep slumbering in his cot,
All wounds and wars and deaths are not. . . .
Such is the household every night
Illumined by the candle light.

Searchlights are so blinding and white,
  The things they show you shall not hear;
Enough to see them ; it is not right
  We should tell of them too, my love, my dear.

In October he was called back home by the sudden death of his only partner, his mother's brother, and was granted three months' special leave. He crowded much strenuous work into that brief space, and in February 1917 rejoined his regiment in England. In May he returned to France, and next month received the M.C. for the brilliant handling of his men in an attack on 14th June near Lens, but he never knew of this honour, for leading his troops—he had now been made acting-captain—in another attack on 1st July he was fatally wounded and taken prisoner, and died the next day. I began speaking of him by quoting some verses in which he seemed calmly to accept as inevitable the certainty of his own death, but his ' In Honorem Fortium ' will tell you that the shadowy premonition that touched him had in it no shadow of fear:

> . . . Grief though it be to die, 'tis grief yet more
> To live and count the dear dead comrades o'er. . . .
>
> Peace. After all, you died not. We've no fear
> But that, long ages hence, you will be near—
> A thought by night—on the warm wind a breath,
> Making for courage, putting by old Death,
> Living wherever men are not afraid
> Of aught but making bravery a parade;
> Yes, parleying with fear, they'll pause and say,
> ' At Gommecourt boys suffered worse that day';
> Or, hesitating on some anxious brink,
> They will become heroic when they think,
> ' Did they not rise mortality above
> Who staked a lifetime all made sweet with love ? '

Grenfell's joy of battle, the high spirits, the courage, and grim, gay humour of our old and new armies, and some of the noblest poetry the war has occasioned live in the two volumes of Ewart Mackintosh who also, as I have shown you, seemed to foresee that he would find his grave in France.

Ewart Alan Mackintosh 137

Born at Brighton, he was a son of the late Alexander Mackintosh, of Alness, in Ross-shire, and a grandson of Dr. Guiness Rogers. At Brighton College he won a St. Paul's scholarship, and in October 1912, says John Murray in a prefatory memoir to *War the Liberator*, went to Christ Church as a classical scholar. He made good there more by his natural capacity than by routine study, developed a passion for poetry and for the arts and traditions of his native Highlands. The war ended his two happy years at Oxford, and before the close of 1914 he was a subaltern of the 5th Seaforths. By the following July he was in the fighting line in France, and in May 1916 received the M.C. for his conduct of a daringly successful raid. Gassed and wounded, he was sent back to England in August, and whilst training cadets at Cambridge became engaged, and had schemes of marrying and settling down in New Zealand after the war. But he could not rest here in safety; he had yearnings to be back with the comrades who had fought beside him and who were carrying on now while he was not there. This feeling is in the poem written at Cambridge, 'From Home'; living at peace he could still hear the roar of the shells, still see the tired patrols out in the rain, and

> The dead men's voices are calling, calling,
> And I must rise and go.

You will understand how irresistible that call was to him if you read his 'In Memoriam' on Private David Sutherland and other of his men who were killed, where, addressing David's father, who mourns the loss of his only son, he sorrows that he, their officer, had fifty such men who followed and trusted him, and it wrung his heart to remember how they had seen him with their dying eyes and held him while they died. I am not quoting from this poem, for it is a tender and poignantly beautiful thing that must be read in its entirety, and it helps one to interpret, if any help be needed, the lines 'To Sylvia,' dated October 1917, when he had had his way and was with the Seaforths in France again, with death waiting him only a month ahead in the battle that was to come near Cambrai:

> God knows—my dear—I did not want
> To rise and leave you so,
> But the dead men's hands were beckoning
> And I knew that I must go.
>
> The dead men's eyes were watching, lass,
> Their lips were asking too:
> We faced it out and paid the price—
> Are we betrayed by you? . . .
>
> But you'll forgive me yet, my dear,
> Because of what you know,
> I can look my dead friends in the face
> As I couldn't two months ago.

V

Mayhap I shall not walk again
  Down Dorset way, down Devon way,
Nor pick a posy in a lane
  Down Somerset and Sussex way;
But though my bones unshriven rot
In some far distant alien spot,
What soul I have shall rest from care
To know that meadows still are fair
  Down Dorset way, down Devon way.
      SERGT. LESLIE COULSON, *From an Outpost.*

BUT all this conscious sacrifice of self must needs have been a small matter if one could have made it without any regrets, without any wistful looking back on happiness forgone and hopes it was hard to relinquish. Making such deliberate renunciation of life and all it meant to them, even for honour and the most sacred cause that ever called for the shedding of blood, these men would have been less admirable, less lovable, less human if they had been touched by no moods in which they knew and felt the full bitterness of it all and could almost find it in their hearts to wish that the cup might pass from them. This mood is a passing cloud over Freston's

> Let's suppose that I am dead,

and over his 'Renunciation':

> Not always do I find myself complain
>   Against this harsh new order of the day,
>   Where we must put the old loved things away
> And rise up to embrace new toil and pain;
> For amongst much of loss there lies much gain:
>   We have learned new strength from learning to obey
>   Necessity; and hearts that used to stray,
> Often too selfishly, are kind again.
> Yet oftentimes to me there cometh one,
>   With sorrow in his eyes, whom half I know:
> Who loved to paint the flowers and the sun
>   In gentle language musically slow:
> Who grieves to leave his life-work scarce begun,
>   Who hoped so much, but now must turn and go.

A passing mood, that works differently on different temperaments, and differently at different times on the same temperament, it edges with mordant irony Alexander

Robertson's 'We shall drink to them that Sleep,' and by turns with irony and with pathos certain of the poems of Leslie Coulson, and his '. . . But a Short Time to Live' with both :

> . . . Our little hour—how short it is
>   When love with dew-eyed loveliness
> Raises her lips for ours to kiss,
>   And dies within our first caress.
> Youth flickers out like wind-blown flame,
>   Sweets of to-day to-morrow sour,
> For time and Death relentless claim
>   Our little hour.
>
> Our little hour—how short a time
>   To wage our wars, to fan our hates,
> To take our fill of armoured crime,
>   To troop our banners, storm the gates :
> Blood on our sword, our eyes blood-red,
>   Blind in our puny reign of power,
> Do we forget how soon is sped
>   Our little hour ?
>
> Our little hour—how soon it dies ;
>   How short a time to tell our beads,
> To chant our feeble litanies,
>   To think sweet thoughts, to do good deeds :

> The altar lights grow pale and dim,
>   The bells hang silent in the tower—
> So passes with the dying hymn
>   Our little hour.

All his love of the open road and the green ways of the English countryside pulses and glows in his song 'From an Outpost':

> I've tramped South England up and down,
>   Down Dorset way, down Devon way,
> Through every little ancient town
>   Down Dorset way, down Devon way:
> I mind the old stone churches there,
> The taverns round the market square,
> The cobbled streets, the garden flowers,
> The sundials telling peaceful hours
>   Down Dorset way, down Devon way . . .

and the joyance and quaintnesses of English country life laugh pleasantly, too, through 'In Abbas Now.' But 'From the Somme,' found on him among his papers after he had fallen in the forefront of a charge against the German position near Lesbœufs, on 7th October 1907, recalls the past delight he had in tramping English highways, loitering through English forest paths, or by the sea, and resting in homely roadside taverns, and realises with a painful intensity that these things are left behind him for ever :

> . . . I played with all the toys the gods provide,
>   I sang my songs and made glad holiday.
> Now I have cast my broken toys aside
>   And flung my lute away.
>
> A singer once, I now am fain to weep,
>   Within my soul I feel strange music swell,
> Vast chants of tragedy too deep—too deep
>   For my poor lips to tell.

There is a stern and darkly passionate protest in the sonnet, ' Judgment,' against the senseless waste and carnage that is making the world desolate, and the same protest is voiced powerfully and as bitterly in ' Who Made the Law ? ' which was also found with his papers after his death :

Who made the Law that men should die in meadows ?
Who spake the word that blood should splash in lanes ?
Who gave it forth that gardens should be boneyards ?
Who spread the hills with flesh, and blood, and brains ?
     Who made the Law ?

Who made the Law that Death should stalk the village ?
Who spake the word to kill among the sheaves ?
Who gave it forth that Death should lurk in hedgerows ?
Who flung the dead among the fallen leaves ?
     Who made the Law ? . . .

But a happier spirit breathes through such lyrics as ' For City Folk ' and ' A Soldier in Hospital,' and ' The Rainbow,' written while he was in the trenches, in France, is filled with a limitless gratitude for the common gifts of life and a sure faith in the budding morrow that the midnight hides :

> I watch the white dawn gleam
>   To the thunder of hidden guns ;
> I hear the hot shells scream
> Through skies as sweet as a dream
>   Where the silver dawnbreak runs ;
> And stabbing of light
> Scorches the virginal white ;
> But I feel in my being the old, high, sanctified thrill,
> And I thank the gods that the dawn is beautiful stiil. . . .

> Where the parapet is low
>   And level with the eye,
> Poppies and cornflowers grow,
> And the corn sways to and fro
>   In a pattern 'gainst the sky ;
> The gold stalks hide
> Bodies of men who died
> Charging at dawn through the dew to be killed or to kill—
> I thank the gods that the flowers are beautiful still.

> When night falls dark we creep
>   In silence to our dead ;
> We dig a few feet deep
> And leave them there to sleep—
>   But blood at night is red,

> Yea, even at night,
> And a dead man's face is white;
> And I dry my hands, that are also trained to kill,
> And I look at the stars—for the stars are beautiful still.

And he wove into his verse something of the dream that is at the hearts of all the fighting-men when he gave language to his never-to-be-realised vision of 'When I Come Home':

> . . . When I come home and leave behind
> Dark things I would not call to mind,
> I'll taste good ale and home-made bread,
> And see white sheets and pillows spread,
> And there is one who'll softly creep
> To kiss me ere I fall asleep
> And tuck me 'neath the counterpane,
> As if I were a boy again,
>   When I come home.
>
> When I come home, from dark to light,
> And tread the roadways long and white,
> And tramp the lanes I tramped of yore,
> And see the village greens once more,
> The tranquil farms, the meadows free,
> The friendly trees that nod to me,
> And hear the lark beneath the sun,
> 'Twill be good pay for what I've done,
>   When I come home.

Always this love for and longing after the quiet country places of little old England—'I have seen men shattered, dying, dead—all the sad tragedy of war,' he said in a letter home, when he was quartered near a devastated French village in July 1916. 'And this murder of old stone and lichened thatches, this shattering of little old churches and homesteads brings the tragedy home to me more acutely. I think to find an English village like this would almost break my heart.'

I knew Leslie Coulson from the days when he was a child in his mother's arms, and it is not easy for me to realise that he grew to manhood, played such a man's part in this war, and had finished with life when he had numbered only half my years. Son of a well-known journalist, he chose journalism as his profession, and after a year or so in the provinces came to London and was rapidly winning recognition as one of the most brilliant of the younger

Leslie Coulson

men. That he was much more than a journalist the few short stories he published and this book of his verse bear witness enough. A month after the declaration of war he enlisted in the 2nd London Regiment of the Royal Fusiliers as a private. 'He was counselled to enter an Officers' Training Corps and obtain a commission,' says his father in a memoir. '"No," he said, "I will do the thing fairly. I will take my place in the ranks." High-minded, conscientious, self-critical, it seemed to him that this was his plain path of duty—to serve as a simple private soldier. He left England with his battalion in December 1914. And none of those to whom he was dear ever saw him again.' From Malta and Egypt he went to Gallipoli, shared in all the horrors of that campaign, and was slightly wounded. 'Never physically robust, he had experienced much ill-health before he became a soldier, and his endurance astonished all who knew him. But after recovery in Egypt from fever—the result of Gallipoli—he rose once again to endure.' By April 1916 he was in France, attached to the 12th London Regiment—the Rangers. 'He was now sergeant, and was recommended for a commission. With his new regiment he took part in the Somme advance on 1st July.' Thenceforward, he was almost continually in the trenches until he fell in action in October. 'He was not by nature a fighter. He was gentle, affectionate, and like all sympathetic natures shrank from inflicting pain. He declared he could never "see red." But he was endowed with the quiet courage and determination that invariably accompany the finer spirit.' Like so many of his comrades, he hated war and its barbarities —' it was just his lion-hearted courage and pride of race that carried him through,' says Major Corbett Smith, who knew him well in the years of peace; 'a sweet and

Howard Stables 151

gallant English gentleman who died that the England he loved might live.' His elder brother, Raymond, a journalist and author as gifted and promising as himself, is a lieutenant now on active service in the Indian Army.

It was while serving with an Indian regiment in Mesopotamia, in the desperate fighting on the road to Kut, that Howard Stables passed beyond human ken. He was reported wounded and missing in February 1917, and it was supposed that he had been taken prisoner at Sanna-i-yat, when the Turks recaptured their first line of trenches there; but after long and exhaustive inquiry the authorities have placed his name on the roll of the dead. Born in 1895, he was educated at St. David's, Reigate, and at Winchester; entered Christ Church College, Oxford, in 1893, and promptly on the coming of war joined the 6th Hampshires, and was sent to India. In 1915 he received his commission in the 5th Gurkha Regiment, and embarked for Mesopotamia :

> Now can we test life's quickness, pay the fee
> For splendid living . . .

he writes in a sonnet ' On leaving India for Mesopotamia.' His letters home show that he took the keenest interest in his work and made light of the difficulties and dangers he had to meet. He was an accomplished musician, and in one letter mentioned that as he had no instrument and could get no music (until one of his Gurkhas, hearing him regret the lack of this, made a native pipe for him) he had taken to writing verses. Presently, he sent a collection of this verse over to Elkin Mathews for publication, but his family knew nothing of his literary projects until the book made its appearance, under the quaint title of *The Sorrow that Whistled*, at the end of 1916. His poems have a strong individual note, and had a very favourable reception at the hands of the

CHARLES HAMILTON SORLEY.
CAPTAIN, SUFFOLK REGT.

reviewers. They are largely a poetical itinerary of his war experiences at home and in the East, with a memory of Winchester, a handful of love poems and two on music. He catches the glamour and magic of the Orient in the best of his verse—in this, for instance, of 'High Barbary':

> The distant mountains' jagged, cruel line
> Cuts the imagination as a blade
> Of dove-grey Damascene. In many a raid
> Here Barbary pirates drave the ships of wine
> Back to Sicilian harbours, harried kine,
> Pillaged Calabrian villages and made
> The land a desolation. . . .
>
> Saracens, Moors, Phœnicians—all the East,
> Franks, Huns, Walloons, the pilgrims of the Pope,
> All, all are gone. The clouds are trailing hence:
> So goes to Benediction some proud priest
> Sweeping the ground with embroidered golden cope.
> —Go, gather up the fumes of frankincense.

Something, too, of the magic and glamour of his alien surroundings he distils into an unpublished poem that sighs with his unsatisfied longing for music :

I have not heard music for so long a time,
For twenty dusty months blown by, and each
    a year
Spent in a dusty prison-house it seems, no
    rhyme,
  No tune to cut the hours upon the walls,
  Only the taunt of fading bugle-calls
To rouse a memory from sleep and make it stir.

Though from red ramparts I can see the city
    swarm
With press of life, look on the swinging caravans
Of camels come from Gwalior beneath the moon,
Hear all the glinting hum of things that take
  The curious fancy, can they ever wake
Those slumbering tunes with all their wealth of
    jewelled fans ?

And shall I hear again the swaying orchestras—
Those rhythmic cohorts—and low passionate songs
    sung
For Sorrow ; the tense preluding of operas
  So rare and fraught ; canorous harmony
  Of bourdons ; airs my mother played to me
And sweet old fiddled strains I knew when I was
    young ? . . .

And from carven doors and lattices, and throng
Of narrow ways that lace the long bazaar's mosaic
Of human hearts and painted curious walls, the song
  Of evening, all the city's tintamar
  Springs up like sandalwood or cinnabar,
A drench of heavy-scented noises, mixed to slake

My thirst for music. Yet right dead I am to all,
Dram-wrapped in unsung harmonies that seem to climb
With cool, slow, rippling strength towards a god's grey hall
  Through wind-swept woods of tonal mysteries,
  Up granite fugues . . . abysmal cadences.—
Ah, I have not heard music for so long a time!

War widened his horizon and took him into new, strange lands that were an unfailing source of interest and delight to him. These and their strangeness and bizarre loveliness were themes that attracted him; only now and then he touched on the war itself, more or less elusively, as in 'Credit and Debit' and 'While Scouring Linen,' or satirically as in 'Thoughts of a Refugee.' He spends no hate or rage on his enemies—I do not remember, indeed, that he ever has anything to say of them. He fought them because they had made that his duty, but he was not inclined to write about them. He had no fear of death, but no love of it. 'Dearest,' he says in the last letter to his mother, written three days before he fell wounded and was no more seen, 'how beautiful a thing life is!'

Perhaps on the dreadful and vaster battlefields of France Death slays such myriads and the menace of it is so constant that there is not often such escape there from the thought of it. Most of the poets who have written from there have been moved to sing of its sadness, its pain, its tragedy, to speculate on it philosophically, to hail it as the honour that shall crown the memory of the brave, or to fling a proud defiance in its face, or to welcome it and hymn its praise as if they looked to rise upon the tomb like triumph on a pedestal. The too-constant presence of Death and the desire for respite is the burden of Victor Ratcliffe's 'Optimism':

At last there'll dawn the last of the long year,
  Of the long year that seemed to dream no end,
Whose every dawn but turned the world more drear
  And slew some hope, or led away some friend.
Or be you dark, or buffeting, or blind,
We care not, Day, but leave not Death behind.

The hours that feed on war go heavy-hearted,
  Death is no fare wherewith to make hearts fain.
Oh, we are sick to find that those who started
  With glamour in their eyes come not again.
O Day, be long and heavy if you will,
But on our hopes set not a bitter heel. . . .

Fell year unpitiful, slow days of scorn,
Your kind shall die, and sweeter days be born.

This is the simple, eternal confession of faith that though the winter is here and has put out the sun and laid the world in ruins, we have only to be patient and the spring will yet return and all be well again. But how is it with those to whom now all seasons are as one? Buried so far from home, with their dearest dreams unsatisfied, do no blind longings reach down to them still and trouble them with vain regrets? A haunting fancy came to Walter Wilkinson, the adopted son of Mrs. William Sharp, that the spring which brought life back to all the earth wakens old yearnings after lost happiness in the dust of his comrades who are dead, and he could hear their voices in the silence:

> Peace! Vex us not—we are the Dead!
> We are the Dead for England slain.
> (O England and the English Spring,
> The English Spring, the Spring-tide rain:
> Ah, God, dear God, in England now!)
> Peace! Vex us not; we are the Dead!
> The snows of Death are on our brow:
>   Peace! Vex us not!
>
> Brothers, the footfalls of the year
> (The maiden month's in England now!)—
> I feel them pass above my head:
> Alas, they echo on my heart!

(Ah, God, dear God, in England now!)—
Peace! Vex me not, for I am dead:
The snows of Death are on my brow:
    Peace! Vex me not!

Brothers, and I—I taste again,
Again I taste the Wine of Spring
(O Wine of Spring and Bread of Love,
O lips that kiss and mouths that sing,
O Love and Spring in England now!)
Peace! Vex me not, but pass above,
Sweet English love, fleet English Spring—
    Peace! Vex me not! . . .

Then the still living man makes answer, urging them to a resigned acceptance of their loss:

> Brothers, I beg you be at rest,
> Be quiet at rest for England's sake.
> The flowerful hours in England now
> Sing low your sleep to English ears;
> And would you have your sorrows wake
> The mother's heart to further tears?—
> Nay, be at peace, her loyal Dead.
>   Sleep! Vex her not!

The pity and tenderness of that are not surpassed in any poem of the war, and the man who wrote it has since made the great acceptance himself—he was killed on Vimy Ridge, and maybe some one of his brothers-in-arms saw him laid to rest with much such thoughts as were his when he witnessed a similar scene and wrote 'The Wayside Burial,' which is dated the 4th April 1917, five days before he died :

They're bringing their recent dead !—No pomp, no
    show :
A dingy khaki crowd—his friends, his own.
I too would like—(God, how that wind does moan !)
To be laid down by friends : it's sweetest so !
A young life, as I take it ; just a lad—
(How cold it blows, and that grey sky how sad !)
And yet : 'For Country'—so a man *should* die :
Comrade unknown, good rest to you !—Good-bye !

They're burying their dead !—I wonder now :
A wife ?—or mother ? Mother it must be,
In some trim home that fronts the English sea
(A sea-coast country ; that the badges show).
And she ?—I sense her grief, I feel her tears :
This, then, the garnered harvest of my years !
And he ?—' For Country, dear, a man *must* die.'
Comrade unknown, good rest to you !—Good-bye !

ALEXANDER ROBERTSON.
CORPL., 12TH YORK AND LANCASTER REGT.

Walter L. Wilkinson

Walter Wilkinson was born at Bristol in 1886. His father, who was chief manager of goods traffic on the Great Western Railway, was an inventive engineer. His mother died when he was a child, and on the death of his father he was introduced to Mrs. William Sharpe, the widow of the well-known author, by Sir Alexander Nelson Hood (Duke of Bronte), who asked her to interest herself in the youngster's striking literary gifts, which, hampered by ill health, he was sedulously developing down to the outbreak of the war. Then, although in peace-time, for the benefit of his health, he had become an expert aeronaut, he was rejected by the Flying Service, solely on the score of his age, and enlisted in the University and Public School Corps as a private in September 1914. Later, he entered the Inns of Court O.T.C., and in 1916 obtained his commission. He was sent to France in January 1917, and within three months was killed in the attack on Vimy Ridge.

It was the voice of the living that cried through Colin Mitchell's 'Autumn in England,' but reading it now is to hear again in fancy that longing of the dead for the England they had loved, for since the spring of 1918 his place has been with them :

Autumn in England ! God ! How my heart cries
Aloud for thee, beloved pearl-gowned bride,
With tresses russet-hued and soft grey eyes
Which sometimes weep and sometimes try to hide
Sweet sadness in a smile of transient bliss,
Painting the West with blushing memories
Of Summer's hot and over-ardent kiss
Betokening farewell. . . .

Autumn in England, why art thou sublime,
So meekly mantled in thy Quaker grey ?
No shining coquetry of tropic clime
Could e'er estrange me, nor could e'er allay
My longing for the country of my birth,
Where winds are passion-voiced, and lullabies
Of raging tempest rock the sons of Earth.
Autumn in England, mine till memory dies !

Sincerity and a simple naturalness of thought and sentiment are the keynotes of Sergeant Colin Mitchell's little collection of verses, *Trampled Clay*. The brotherly regard that has grown up betwixt officers and men whose days are bounded by the common peril of the trenches is in the breezy, rugged story of 'Our Captain'; there is naked realism and power in the thumb-nail battle-sketch 'Hooge'; charm in the brief idyll of 'Hughine and Ninette'; the boyish fun of the regiment in 'Soliloquies on the March'; and in others are a man's unpretentious musings on life and death and the ways of God, and a sorrow for the dead and for those who will miss them.

The wonder is that so much verse by soldier poets, written on active service, posted to friends at home, or stowed away in a man's kit, or in his pockets, and often found on him or among his belongings only after he was dead, has survived all the chances of loss or destruction and arrived at ultimate preservation in print. The wonder, too, is not that some of such verse, scribbled down in odds and ends of time, under all manner of inconveniences and discouragements and amidst the grimmest preoccupations, should be halting and flawed in utterance, but that so much of it should be so careful of form and finish as it is. Through the kindness of his brother, the worn, red-covered pocket-book that J. W. Streets carried with him on his campaigning has come into my hands. There are jottings in it of stray ideas or phrases that occurred to him for stories or for verses, and on certain of its pages, or on loose leaves folded in between them, are various poems, two or three of which have not been included in his published volume. They all bear marks of haste, are in pencil and often difficult to read, and show little sign of revision. Two of these unpublished poems are characteristic of the high idealism and the spirit of mystical exaltation in which he entered upon the war. All his beliefs, all his instincts were opposed to it, and nothing but the martyrdom of Belgium, and a burning love of his own country and of the peace and liberty that must be saved from the menace of the Hun could ever have made a soldier of him. What death in such causes meant to him glimmers upon you from 'The Vigil':

> Sentry, what do you see out there ?—
> Sorrow, mourning, everywhere,
> Death in youth, and stranger things,
> Yet dawn appearing on wild, swift wings.
>
> Sentry, what do you see out there ?
> Youth grown old, and Spring grown sere,
> Life a bitter memory,
> Love a dark Gethsemane.
>
> Sentry, what do you see out there ?
> Madness, chaos, everywhere,
> Men entwined in sanguine strife,
> Yet Youth in Calvary finding Life.

—it rings like a trumpet-call in the second of these unpublished poems, 'The Fallen':

Their laughter and their merriment have ceased ;
Their dreams have found Life's winter in the bud ;
The cycle of their life, its dawn decreased
Ere Love had sung the matin-song ; their good
Was in the embryo, lips had scarcely known
The first mad kiss of love, scarce felt the thrill
Of woman's hair and cheek ; their dreams had grown
Not yet to fadeless purpose, tireless will.

There is a dawn whose flush outlives the day,
Engraves itself upon the consciousness :
There is a fate that Youth will gladly pay
So honour flourish, beauty grow no less :
To Liberty their heritage they gave
And won immortal glory at the grave.

Streets was a coal miner, and quitted work in the pit to be one of 'Kitchener's men.' J. M., a schoolmaster and mission worker, who was a friend of his, writes in a postscript to 'The Undying Splendour,' that 'born in the same village, attending the same Sunday School, playing in the same cricket team, finally coming to intimacy, the ideals and pursuits of J. W. S. flowed into our common chat. Condemned, as he was, to toil from boyhood in the mine, and also to environment that wounded his sensitive nature, his was yet ever the search after the beautiful and the true.' He was a keen helper in the work of ' the small Wesleyan community of his village,' and ' early, too, he tried to express himself with the brush, and gave great promise, though always the call of a written mode of expressing himself was with him. . . . His poems tell the secret of his whole life, which was an untiring love of nature,' and there is one line from them, says this friend,

  O Liberty, at thy command, we challenge Death,

which ' tells in essence the reason that led one who hated war to go from that quiet North Derbyshire village to make one of the millions who are fighting for us and our

Allies.' From the training camp at Hurdcott, from the trenches in France, he sent home his poems from time to time, pencilled on scraps of paper, and looked to revising them in proof, but he was reported wounded and missing in July 1916, and the following May, while his book was in the press, it was officially notified that he had been killed.

In a letter to Galloway Kyle, enclosing the sonnet sequence, 'The Undying Splendour,' which was to give the title to his volume, Streets offers this apologia and explanation: 'They were inspired while I was in the trenches, where I have been so busy I have had little time to polish them. I have tried to picture some thoughts that pass through a man's brain when he dies. I may not see the end of the poems, but hope to live to do so. We soldiers have our views of life to express, though the boom of death is in our ears. We try to convey something of what we

ERIC FITZWATER WILKINSON.
CAPTAIN, WEST YORKS (LEEDS RIFLES).

feel in this great conflict to those who think of us, and sometimes, alas! mourn our loss. We desire to let them know that in the midst of our keenest sadness for the joy of life we leave behind, we go to meet death grim-lipped, clear-eyed, and resolute-hearted.' Which merely reflects the man as he reveals himself, without premeditation, in his verses; and there is testimony to the truth of the picture in a note from his company officer, Captain Moore. . . . 'When he was reported missing, few of us who knew him had much hope of seeing him again. We knew that Streets was not the man easily to surrender': and in a letter from Major Plackett, under whom Streets served in England, in Egypt and, to the last, in France: . . . 'He died as he had lived—a man. If his verses are as good as his reputation as a soldier, you may rest assured that the book will be a great success.'

Some of us used to say, perhaps too complacently, that Waterloo was won on the playing-fields of Eton. Be that as it may, it is clear to all eyes that the greater, more terrible battles of this war were won on the playing-fields and in the class-rooms of the Council Schools, as well as of the Colleges, and in the homes of the whole nation —in cottages and workmen's dwellings no less than in town and country mansions. The Public School spirit is a splendid and a potent tradition, but it does not account for such men as Streets and, in our days, there are not a few of them. I honour their memories too profoundly to think for a moment that it was just their Public School training which made such dear and heroic souls as Grenfell, Philipps, Palmer, or Wyndham Tennant the fearless and perfect gentle knights that they were; for without that training at least as many have risen, like Ledwidge from his scavengering, like Flower from his clerking,

William Ambrose Short

like Streets from toiling in the mine, fired by the same shining ideals, the same hatred of cruelty and scorn of wrong, the same selfless love of country, and have died for these things with a chivalry and courage that are of no school but of all schools, that are of no class, no limited section of the community, but are in the very blood and bones of our people, in the large tradition of the race. Whatever else the war may have to teach us, this it has taught us already, for it is the emergence in rich and poor, plebeian and aristocrat, of fundamental qualities which are the natural heritage of all that has drawn us together and brought us to a recognition of our common brotherhood.

This good sense of brotherhood, at all events between officers and men, runs pleasantly through the verse of Lieutenant-Colonel Short, who was killed in France in June 1917; it is in his warm-hearted response on receipt of a Christmas card from the Sergeants' Mess of his battery, and you glimpse it in and between the lines of other of his poems. He was of the Old Army, and in character and temperament had much in common with Brian Brooke. There is sometimes a sombre touch, but always a sturdy, breezy, soldierly courage in his war verse and often a delightfully whimsical humour. Perhaps one lingers most over the tender, fanciful series to his wife, and especially over the three charmingly playful poems to his baby daughter on her birthdays, the second of which—

> My little lady now that you are two—

was written in an interval of fighting on the retreat from Mons. He is so genially frank and unaffected that, after reading his posthumous volume, you feel you have become as intimate with the man himself, the brave, gracious, friendly spirit of him, as if you had known him personally.

VI

> Come home!—Come home!
> The winds are at rest in the restful trees,
> At rest are the waves of the sundown seas;
> And home—they're home—
> The wearied hearts and the broken lives—
>   At home! At ease!
>   LIEUT. WALTER L. WILKINSON, *At Last Post*.

CLIFFORD FLOWER, to whom a few lines back I made casual reference, was a Leeds boy, who began life at the age of thirteen and a half in the office of a local firm of Iron and Steel Tube manufacturers. He had been promoted to the Drawing Office of the firm's headquarters at Birmingham, and was in his twenty-third year when Germany invaded Belgium. No sooner were Kitchener's posters calling from walls and hoardings for volunteers than he offered himself for enlistment, and was rejected. He tried to dodge in at two or three other recruiting depôts, but was consistently barred out by them all because he was half an inch short of the standard military height. But the youngster who, a year before, could pour such a passion of sympathy for the Black Country strikers into his verses, 'My People's Voice,' could not be deaf to Belgium's greater agony, and he was too bent on doing his duty to be easily baulked. He wrote to Lord Kitchener direct, says the memoir which prefaces the privately printed sheaf of his verse, and 'stated his case as to how he had presented himself for enlistment at various recruiting offices and been rejected every time owing to a slight shortness of height. He concluded his letter thus: "My Lord, I have answered *your* appeal, will you answer *mine*?" It cannot be said that the letter ever reached Lord Kitchener, but a reply came from the War Office by return of post, enclosing a sealed document which he was instructed to deliver to the recruiting officer. It was an order to "Enlist the bearer, Clifford Flower, at once."' And it worked like magic. Without any further examination, he was passed as a private into the 2nd Battalion of the Warwickshire Regiment, but got himself transferred to the Royal Field Artillery. 'Three weeks after joining, he was offered a stripe on the condition that he joined the clerical staff, but this he declined, preferring to rough it with the ordinary Tommies.' Rough it he did out in France during the first year of the war, but, cheerful and a sturdy optimist, he ignored his hardships in his letters or made a jest of them. Most of his verse dates from his civilian days; of the four poems he wrote at the front, two are in a lighter vein, blithely anticipating peace, and commemorating the luck of his battery; one calls upon Red, the king of colours, to pay homage henceforth to Khaki; and the fourth, 'A Calm Night at the Front,' sketches the scene around him and the thoughts that it stirs in him:

> . . . The rifle fire has died away,
>   All silent now: the moon on high
> Would set a truce until the day,
>   God staying the hand of destiny. . . .
>
> O womenfolk of British lands,
>   Who toil and sweat in holiest cause,
> Oh raise in prayer your clasped hands
>   That men may see the curse of wars.
>
> A single star-light held in space
>   Has filled the trench with radiance white,
> A cautious soldier hides his face,
>   Somebody's calling, so good-night.

He took a shrapnel wound in his left arm as buoyantly as he took every other trouble that came his way, and remained on duty. Nominally a driver, for the last eighteen months of his service he was on the signalling staff. On Easter Sunday 1917 he was one of three signallers who volunteered to accompany an infantry battalion in the advance towards Lens and

RICHARD DENNYS.
CAPTAIN, LOYAL NORTH LANCS. REGT.

at six in the morning went over the top with them in a blinding snowstorm. At Easter in the year before the war he had returned home from Birmingham, and described his delight in that home-coming very simply and vividly in 'Easter—Home Again':

The wheels of the train sing a full-toned song
As they rattle the hours of waiting along,
And soon I am swinging across the street
To the rhythm of joy which my pulses beat,
To arrive at the gate, which creaks as of old ;
Its bars of iron seem like pillars of gold
Flashing behind as I leap to the top
Of the clean-scoured steps then, brought to a stop,
I ring at the bell, give the firm hand to Len,
And I 'm fast in your arms and home again !

It might well have stood as a snapshot of his home-coming from France, but he was not to return from there. On 20th April, he was in a dug-out in the lines that had been newly captured from the enemy when a German shell thundered at the entrance and he was instantly killed.

Born in the same year as Flower, Eric Fitzwater Wilkinson embarked for France early in 1915 as a lieutenant in the Leeds Rifles, and within a few months won the M.C. for bringing in wounded under fire. He was educated at Dorchester and Ilkley Grammar Schools and, having gained scholarships, went to Leeds University for a three years' engineering course, and joined the O.T.C. there. Presently, he became a junior master in his old school at Ilkley, and his contributions of verse, serious and humorous, to the school magazine intimate that his bent was not exclusively towards engineering. Having passed his intermediate B.A. (London) examination with honours, he was preparing for his final when, as with so many others, the war put an end to his plans. After a year of hard fighting in the Ypres trenches, he was appointed town mayor of Varennes, and had risen to the rank of captain when he was killed ' very gallantly leading his company' in the attack on Passchendaele Ridge. Writing to his mother on the eve of that action a letter that reached her when he was dead, he tells her that, apart from 'a shrinking of the nerves which I always have to conquer, I can honestly say that I have not the slightest fear of death in me, which makes it vastly easier.' Which is in keeping with the lines on 'Death,' where he turns from his question indifferently and sees how a man may find life in losing it :

> What is it ? Though it come swiftly and sure
>   Out of the dark womb of fate,
> What that a man cannot dare and endure,
>   Level heart steady, eyes straight ? . . .
>
> The fight shall roll o'er us—a broad crimson tide,
>   Feet stamp, shells wail, bullets hiss,
> And England be greater because we have died :
>   What end can be finer than this ?

And he dedicates himself to death for the victory of right over wrong with a note of still loftier triumph in 'To My People before the Great Offensive,' offering comfort to those whose son he is and bidding them not to sorrow overmuch for him if he falls—

If then, amidst some millions more, this heart
  Should cease to beat,

Mourn not for me too sadly; I have been
For months of an exalted life, a King;
Peer for these months of those whose graves grow
    green
Where'er the borders of our Empire fling
Their mighty arms. And if the crown is death,
Death while I 'm fighting for my home and king,
Thank God the son who drew from you his breath
  To death could bring

A not entirely worthless sacrifice,
Because of those brief months when life meant more
Than selfish pleasures. Grudge not then the price,
But say, ' Our country in the storm of war
Has found him fit to fight and die for her,'
And lift your hearts in pride for evermore.
But when the leaves the evening breezes stir
  Close not the door,

For if there 's any consciousness to follow
The deep, deep slumber that we know as Death,
If Death and Life are not all vain and hollow,
If life is more than so much indrawn breath,
Then in the hush of twilight I shall come—
One with immortal Life that knows not Death
But ever changes form—I shall come home ;
   Although beneath

A wooden cross the clay that once was I
Has ta'en its ancient earthy form anew,
But listen to the wind that hurries by,
To all the song of Life for tones you knew :
For in the voice of birds, the scent of flowers,
The evening silence and the falling dew,
Through every throbbing pulse of nature's powers
   I 'll speak to you.

It were easy enough to write so courageously of dying and play with fancies of what may happen after death if, writing as a distant onlooker and in no danger, one merely dramatised the thoughts and emotions of the men who were in the battle lines ; but the strength and glory of these soldier poets is that they wrote in the heart of darkness, that the terrors they clothed in beauty were storming round about them, that they were fronting the bitter death they felt they were doomed to die and welcomed in their songs, and that they justified in action the highest and proudest of their written words. They could look forward without a tremor, and if they could not always glance back without regret it was because the sacrifice they were making was a very real one—they were all young, life was sweet to them and had been rich in promise; yet they had it in them to subdue themselves and trample their regrets unflinchingly underfoot, upheld by the faith that they gave their lives that the world might remain worth living in for the rest of us.

That is the feeling, plainly expressed or implicit, in so much that the soldier poets have written of the war. To turn for a moment from the poets to a prose writer—it is the feeling, the desire that speaks to you from the letters of Harold Chapin, who was on the high road to success as a dramatist when, after attending classes in first aid, he enlisted in the R.A.M.C. on the 2nd September 1914, to be killed at the battle of Loos, on the 26th September, a year later. So far as I know, he wrote nothing in verse, but there is the truest poetry of idea and of emotion in certain of his plays. American by birth, he had lived many years in England and done the best of his work here, but it was not for England only that he went into the war. Nor was he out after the quickest peace of any sort that would last his time. He thought less of his own future than of the future of his little son, and contemplating the likelihood of his not returning, he writes more than once of what he would wish his son to be taught, and not to be taught, when he is old enough. 'Have I warned you against rumours?' he says in a letter from the front to his wife.

'Yes, I believe I have. Beware of them, especially rumours of peace. We don't want peace till they 're beaten, do we?' And to his mother, in June 1915: 'I made the discovery yesterday that unless I can leave a nice, well-finished-off war behind me I don't want to come home. This in spite of the fact that I am regularly and miserably homesick for at least half an hour every morning and two hours every evening, and heartily fed up with the war every waking hour in between. . . . To go home to Vallie and Mummy is not what I want yet. I want from the bottom of my heart to see it out'; and to his mother again a week later: 'Don't listen to peace talk yet—discourage it if you can. Nothing makes us madder out here. Remember we are on the wrong side of the top to talk of peace. It is a worse idea than the war. A patch-up peace with those bloody gentry over there!' This was a man at the front who wrote that, and added, 'Do you realise that I can see one of them now? ... I can hear them in the distance too. ... No peace until we are on top, please.' It is the home-staying pacifist, claiming to be more humane than such men as these, who clamours incessantly for peace by immediate negotiation because, forsooth, as he speciously reiterates, peace will have to be made by negotiation at last—as if it made no difference whether you tried to reason with your enemy while he had his foot on your neck or after you were well on your feet again and at no such disadvantage.

There is a passage in Dixon Scott's *Men of Letters,* in an essay on Rupert Brooke—almost the last literary work that he did—which chimes with the songs of our poet soldiers and has always seemed to me to embody the motives, the ideals, often inarticulate, that, in the main, prompted our younger generation, as they prompted him, to their impetuous defence of the rights of every man against the outrageous brigandage of the Hun. Loathing war and unable to imagine, as he told me, that he could ever really bring himself to ' stick a man,' he joined up at once and was already a lieutenant of artillery when he wrote this essay, in which he says that for him Brooke's sonnet commencing,

> If I should die think only this of me,

captured completely ' one of the dimmest and deepest, one of the most active but most elusive, of all the many mixed motives, beliefs, longings, ideals, which make those of us who have flung aside everything in order to fight still glad and gratified that we took the course we did. There do come moments, I must admit,' he adds, ' when doubts descend on one dismally, when one's soldiering seems nothing but a contemptible vanity, indulged in largely to keep the respect of lookers-on. And, of course, cowardice of that sort, a small pinch of it anyway, did help to make most of us brave. There was the love of adventure, too, the longing to be in the great scrum—the romantic appeal of " the neighing steed and the shrill trump "— all the glamour and illusion of the violent thing that has figured for ever in books, paintings and tales, as the supreme earthly adventure. . . . But beneath all these impulses, like a tide below waves, there lies also a world of much deeper emotion. It is a love of peace, really, a delight in fairness and faith—an inherited joy in all the traditional graces of life and in all the beauty that has been blessed by affection. It is an emotion, an impulse, for which the word " patriotism " is a term far too simple and trite. . . . One fights for the sake of happiness—for one's own happiness first of all, certain that did one not fight one would be miserable for ever—and then, in the second place, for the quiet solace and pride of those others, spiritual and mental sons of ours, if not actually physical—the men of our race who will depend for so much of their dignity upon the doings of the generation before. War is a boastful, beastly business; but if we don't plunge into it now we lower the whole pitch of posterity's life, leave them with only some dusty relics of racial honour. To enter into this material hell now is to win for our successors a kind of immaterial heaven. There will be an ease and a splendour in their attitude towards life which a peaceful hand now would destroy. It is for the sake of that spiritual ease and enrichment of life that we fling everything aside now to learn to deal death.'

This is why he and thousands of his fellows went to war—not for the glory of conquest and with insane ambitions of world power—but for love of peace and honour and freedom, and that it might not be said of them that they had betrayed posterity into bondage. After all, there are dearer things than life, things without which life is not worth having; and in this knowledge Scott laid down his own at Gallipoli in October 1915.

In the same month of that year, a kindred spirit, Charles Hamilton Sorley, was killed in action at Hullach; and look what a little thing he could make of the death he was to die:

> All the hills and vales along
> Earth is bursting into song,
> And the singers are the chaps
> Who are going to die, perhaps.
>   Oh sing, marching men,
>   Till the valleys ring again.
>   Give your gladness to earth's keeping,
>   So be glad when you are sleeping.
>
> Cast away regret and rue,
> Think what you are marching to.
> Little live, great pass.
> Jesus Christ and Barabbas
> Were found the same day.
> This died, that went his way.

> So sing with joyful breath.
> For why, you are going to death.
> Teeming earth will surely store
> All the gladness that you pour. . . .
>
> From the hills and valleys earth
> Shouts back the sound of mirth,
> Tramp of feet and lilt of song
> Ringing all the road along.
> All the music of their going,
> Ringing swinging glad song-throwing,
> Earth will echo still, when foot
> Lies numb and voice mute.
> > On, marching men, on
> > To the gates of death with song.
> > Sow your gladness for earth's reaping,
> > So you may be glad, though sleeping.
> > Strew your gladness on earth's bed,
> > So be merry, so be dead.

Here, in a splendour of bizarre metaphysical fantasy, is the rapt sense of mystical joy in dying for a great end that shines through Grenfell's ' Into Battle,' and Rupert Brooke's

> If I should die think only this of me :
> That there 's some corner of a foreign land
> That is for ever England . . .

and is the prevailing note in the poems of J. W. Streets, whose love of life is so intense that he never doubts but he shall pick up the thread of it again on the other side of night :

> And if thy twilight fingers round me steal
> And draw me unto death—thy votary
> Am I. O Life, reach out thy hands to me.

This same ecstasy thrills in his many references to the privilege of offering up one's youth on the altar for the realisation of a noble purpose :

> The soul of life is in the will to give
> The best of life in willing sacrifice :
> Youth only reaches greatness when he dies
> In fullest prime that love and truth may live.

' Youth's Consecration ' is achieved when he has gladly sacrificed himself for the salvation of freedom :

> Lovers of Life, we pledge thee, Liberty,
> And go to death calmly, triumphantly.

Christ taught us to succour need and ' led the way to Life—to Sacrifice ' :

O Thou who pleaded ever 'mid disdain
That when for weaker comrades we did give
Our own sweet lives, alone then did we live—
Know Thou, O Christ, Thou didst not live in vain,
For youth hath found in Love vitality
And treads with thee the way to Calvary.

His ' Triumph ' is that ' feeling the presage of the unborn years,' Youth will

  Brave the dark confines
And wrest from Death his diadem of tears,

and that though he should die in Belgium he will have no regret nor dream that his Youth has been in vain, knowing still ' that Love its life in death can find '; and his requiem over the dead is a rejoicing :

For these like some great planet spheric-whirled
Have swung into the orbit of a greater world.
These topped the hill of Youth ; stood on the verge
Of vision ; saw within the furthest star
Spiritual presences, Love's own avatar ;
These the twin worlds of soul and flesh did merge
Into a dream, a consciousness that stole
Around their spirits like an aureole.

He hails the dead as

> Youth triumphant, greater than his fate;

and elsewhere exults that he and his comrades, dying, will have given their all, even their heritage of youth, that the reign of humanity shall be restored:

> We march to death singing our deathless songs,
> Like knights invested with a purpose high,

and foresees how the youth of the years to be

> Will hear our phantom armies marching by,

and learn from them how to die for liberty.

No militarism is here, nor in any of the poems I have read by these soldiers; no strut of the goose-step, no taste for slaughter nor lust of conquest for its own sake, nor any of the cheap, dazzling blatancies that belong to the militaristic spirit. These men were too sanely human to cherish hatred except of war and the folly or mad ambition of those who had plunged the world into it. Streets at one end of our social scale is not more passionate in his love of humanity, his detestation of the wrong and brutality of war and the silly desire for such glory as it can give than, at the other, was the younger son of the Earl of Selborne, Captain the Hon. Robert Palmer, who died a wounded prisoner in the hands of the Turk, and in the year before his death made this his battle prayer :

How long, O Lord, how long before the flood
Of crimson-welling carnage shall abate ?
From sodden plains in West and East the blood
Of kindly men streams up in mists of hate
Polluting Thy clean air ; and nations great
In reputation of the arts that bind
The world with hopes of Heaven, sink to the state
Of brute barbarians, whose ferocious mind
Gloats o'er the bloody havoc of their kind,
Not knowing love nor mercy. Lord, how long
Shall Satan in high places lead the blind
To battle for the passions of the strong ?
Oh touch Thy children's hearts, that they may know,
Hate their most hateful, pride their deadliest foe.

Charles Hamilton Sorley

Staying in Germany, a month before the war, Charles Sorley wrote that though there was a type of German who had been ruined by Sedan he liked the German nature, 'as far as it is not warped by the German Empire.' After war had commenced and he was in the army, he says, 'I think the Kaiser not unlike Macbeth, with the military clique in Prussia as his Lady Macbeth, and the court flatterers as the weird sisters'; and in another letter he thinks 'a close parallel may be drawn between Faust and present history' (with Germany as Faust and Belgium as Gretchen). 'And Faust found spiritual salvation in the end!' At the outset, before the Hun had proved himself by such appalling inhumanities as sink him below the level of aboriginal negroes, Sorley could find it in his heart to write a largely tolerant, compassionate sonnet 'To Germany,' commiserating her and ourselves on the woe that had overwhelmed both:

> You were blind like us. Your hurt no man designed
> And no man claimed the conquest of your land.
> But gropers both through fields of thought confined
> We stumble, and we do not understand. . . .

And Alexander Robertson, finding on the body of a dead German soldier a prayer-book, letters, and photographs of wife and children, writes pityingly in 'Thou Shalt Love Thine Enemies':

> They were not meant for our too curious eyes
> Or our imaginations to surmise
> From what they tell much that they leave untold.
> Strangers and foemen we, yet we behold,
> Sad and subdued, thy solace and thy cheer. . . .

When you know something of Alexander Robertson, scholarly, peace-loving, high-minded, you recognise how unselfconsciously he has revealed his personality in the verse he has written. He was born at Edinburgh in 1882; had a brilliant career at school and college, winning at

Edinburgh University medals in Latin, Education, and Political Economy. He took his M.A. degree there, with a First Class Honours in History. Then for three years he taught, as senior master in History, at his old school, George Watson's College, Edinburgh. He also taught in a French Lycée at Caen, and attended the university of that city. But feeling that school-teaching narrowed his sphere too much, he gave it up, and went for three years to Oxford. 'With his scholarly tendencies and aspirations, these were very happy years to him,' says his brother, Dr. Niven Robertson, 'as the tenor of the poems in *Comrades* show. He spent most of his time in historical research, and gained the B.Litt. of Oxford. The subject of his thesis was *The Life of Sir Robert Moray*. This is to be published in book form, but its publication has been delayed by the war. By those who are able to judge he was regarded as one who would, sooner or later, make his name as a historian, but this was not to be.'

In September 1914 he enlisted as a private, joining from a sincere sense of duty only, as he had no inclination to fighting—his whole life had been devoted to study; he had never cared for sport or strenuous doings of any but a studious sort; and he could not but have wistful memories, such as came to him 'On Passing Oxford in a Troop Train':

> . . . Away with memories? Yet there's one
> I fain would keep till life be done;
> No pining for a vanished bliss
> Which once we had but now we miss—
> Such is the comfort of the weak;
> The strong another solace seek;
> New circumstance alone can bring
> Fresh outlook and imagining.
> So that dear mother of the soul
> Who found us sick and made us whole
> Restrained not but enjoined the quest
> Of Truth until the final rest,
> And hinted that the search might be
> The object of eternity;

> That in defiance and in hope
> Alone may lie the means to cope
> With what life brings of ill; that naught
> Is failure but despairing thought.
> Him who remembers this the years
> Can bring no too triumphant fears
> Nor the stern future's gaze appal,
> Mysterious-eyed, inimical.

War could have no possible attractions for a man of his intellectual aims and gracious personal character. ' When he entered the Army he sacrificed all his joy of life in the world of intellectual pursuits,' but the great mood in which the sacrifice was made is in that verse of his. The love of culture remained with him even in the midst of army life, when there was little time or privacy to foster it, and in Egypt, where he went with his battalion in December 1915, he gave the leisure he could get from railway making and trench digging to the study of Italian. His regiment was transferred to France in April 1916, and after a spell in hospital, with epidemic jaundice, he was glad to rejoin his old university comrades in the front line near Albert, early in June. On the morning of 1st July, in the great offensive on the Somme, he died along with several of those comrades in the very forefront of our attack on the German position. All his poems were written while he was on active service. 'It was his greatest joy and a great solace to him,' writes his brother, 'to express his soul in them, as army life was far from congenial to a man of his character.' Like his 'Moses on Pisgah,' he saw far off the land of promise he was not to tread. Strife and bloodshed were around him, but his dreams were not of them—always, as in the hospital at Provence, he was grateful for a window, a small space, through which he could yet see nature and humanity. His vision of the 'Survivors,' who shall reach the goal, sees them looking back with sadness on

Photo by Wykeham.

FRANCIS ST. VINCENT MORRIS.
LIEUT., 3RD SHERWOOD FORESTERS (ATTACHED R.F.C.).

the dark hours when necessity made them blind to pity, as to danger,

> Our human kind
> Debasing to an instrument to slay
> Man and his hopes ;

and the reward that is to be theirs for all they have done and endured is not the crushing of their enemy, the conquest of his land, but to live their own lives once more, to have

> Self-mastery again, once more the sweet
> Beatitude of freedom and the sense
> Of quiet and security, intense ;
> Home and home faces lit with unexpressed
> Joy, and the gladness of the spirit's rest.

Less of a student, perhaps, more of a man of action, Lieutenant A. L. Jenkins was still a dreamer, an idealist, whose ideal of happiness was not of a kind that could ever be won by the sword, but is the strange, sweet, immaterial something that he sighs after in ' Forlorn

Adventurers,' the lyric that lends its title to his book :

> . . . The sweetest love of the loves of earth,
>   Treasure thrice tried in fire,
> Power beyond the dreams of kings—
> These we have got in our venturings,
>   But never our heart's desire.
>
> And of such spoil we are content
>   Our loves alone to keep :
> Gold through our careless hands shall run,
> And all the lands we lightly won
>   Wiser than we shall reap.
>
> Wayfaring men, yea, fools are we,
>   Who do not count the cost :
> Of little worth in men's esteem,
> Yet happy, for we chase a dream
>   More fair than aught we lost.

The eldest son of Sir John Lewis Jenkins, K.C.S.I., I.C.S., he had himself hoped to enter the Indian Civil Service, ' for which,' writes Frank Fletcher, in an introduction to *Forlorn Adventurers*, ' he seemed naturally destined by the traditions of both sides of his family and by his father's brilliant record.' Another Marlborough boy, he went to Balliol with a classical scholarship, but abandoned all personal ambitions, and became a lieutenant in the Duke of Cornwall's Light Infantry in 1914. He served for a year in India, and then went in charge of a machine-gun section to Aden, and his recollections of campaigning there are in ' Arabia,' written just before he left Aden for Palestine :

> An aching glare, a heat that kills,
>   Skies hard and pitiless overhead,
> And, overmastering lesser ills,
>   Sad bugles keening comrades dead :
> Fever and dust and smiting sun,
>   In sooth a land of little ease :
> Yet, now my service here is done,
>   I think on other things than these.
>
> Dawn on the desert's short-lived dew,
>   Blue shadows on the silver sand,
> Grey shimmering mists that still renew
>   The magic of the hinterland :

Sunsets ablaze with crimson fire,
  Pale moons like plates of beaten gold,
Soft nights that fevered limbs desire,
  And stars whereto our stars are cold :

Sharp, rattling fights at peep of day,
  Machine-guns searching scrub and plain,
Red lances questing for the prey,
  And kites quick stooping to the slain :
Swift shifting stroke and counter-stroke,
  Advance unhurrying and sure,
Until the stubborn foeman broke—
  These are the memories that endure. . . .

His section being disbanded, he joined the Royal Flying Corps, trained in Egypt, returned to England, and while serving in a home-defence squadron was killed in an aeroplane accident on the last night of 1917. That he too knew for what he died and was more than willing to die for it let his ' Happy Warriors,' an elegy on his dead friends who had fallen in battle bear witness :

Surely they sleep content, our valiant dead,
   Fallen untimely in the savage strife :
They have but followed whither duty led,
   To find a fuller life.

Who, then, are we to grudge the bitter price
   Of this our land inviolate through the years,
Or mar the splendour of their sacrifice
   That is too high for tears. . . .

God grant we fail not at the test—that when
   We take, mayhap, our places in the fray,
Come life, come death, we quit ourselves like men,
    The peers of such as they.

The gallantry and glamour of old wars is in his 'Crusaders,' written in Palestine, and the one dread that, as in the verse of Major Stewart and others, haunted these brave men—the fear of being afraid—is in his finely impressive lyric, 'Fear'; but an eager joy in the charm and loveliness of the kindlier, sweeter ways of the world blows like a wind of morning through his before the war 'Song of the Road,' 'The Land of Dreams,' and 'In Praise of

Devon'; and in one of the last of his poems, 'Bondage,' you see that, like Robertson, he was not fighting for any vain glory of conquest:

> Oh, I am sick of ways and wars
>   And the homeless ends of the earth,
> I would get back to the northern stars
>   And the land where I had birth,
> And take to me a dainty maid,
>   And a tiny patch of ground,
> Where I may watch small green things grow
>   And the kindly months come round. . . .
>
> The wine of war is bitter wine,
>   And I have drunk my fill;
> My heart would seek its anodyne
>   In homely things and still. . . .

If I have stressed this essentially human note, it is because it is so implicit and insistent in the songs that the soldier poets of this war have sung. They went into battle soberly or with a mystical exultation, prepared to die in it, but with a will to victory for the sake of peace and right and with a settled courage that nothing could shake. They descended into the pit and fought with beasts, but remained unconquerably human. Noel Hodgson, coming out of the desperate fighting at Loos, wrote on his way back to the rest camp :

> We that have seen the strongest
>   Cry like a beaten child,
> The sanest eyes unholy,
>   The cleanest hands defiled ;
> We that have known the heart-blood
>   Less than the lees of wine,
> We that have seen men broken,
>   We know man is divine.

And Dennys, when his death was imminent, sent up from amidst the carnage and desolation a vastly different message than that which Achilles shouted over his trenches :

> But now I know that nought is purposeless,
>   And, even in destruction, we can find
> A power whose steady motive is to bless
>   The ultimate redemption of mankind. . . .

> Ours is the privilege of sacrifice,
>   And cheerfully we heap the sacred pyre,
> Our willing selves the offering—the price
>   Demanded to make fierce the cleansing fire.
>
> Ourselves we set the light, and know it wise,
>   (Seek not, O faint of heart, our hands to stay),
> That, phoenix-like, a nobler world may rise
>   From out the ashes of a dead to-day.

Belief in a divinity that is shaping the rough-hewn brutalities of war to beneficent ends breaks as clearly from 'The Shrine,' one of Eugene Crombie's poems:

> . . . Returning through the woods at evening's hour
> I lay before Thy shrine my offering,
> My candle-flame a yellow crocus flower,
> Its life but newly lit, to Thee I bring,
> In thanks that I can see Thy guiding hand
> In every flower that decorates the land.

He wrote this at his billet in France shortly before he marched out to the attack in which he fell. Surely, it is more wonderful that he, and others with him, could hold by such faith there, where the vast menace of death was close about them, than that the saint of old, in no

Photo by Keogh Bros.

T. M. KETTLE.
LIEUT., DUBLIN FUSILIERS.

Cyril William Winterbotham

immediate peril, should be able to say, 'Though He slay me, yet will I trust Him.'

And faith as unquenchable is characteristic of Cyril Winterbotham, especially of his last poems, 'A Christmas Prayer from the Trenches,' and 'The Cross of Wood,' the latter written a month before he was killed in action. He had written verses since his childhood, and the early poems gathered into his little volume show a delightful sense of humour and a real love of nature. From Cheltenham College he went to Oxford in 1906; and in 1911 he was called to the Bar. He was keenly interested in politics, and in 1913 was adopted as prospective Liberal candidate for East Gloucestershire. His warmest sympathies went out to the poor and unfortunate, and he gave much of his time to useful work with the Oxford and Bermondsey Mission. In September 1914 he obtained a commission in the 1/5 Gloucestershire Regiment, and was in

Flanders and France from March 1915 until his death. 'He was essentially a man of peace,' writes his mother, 'and had a horror of war and bloodshed, but when the call came he did not hesitate—every other feeling gave way to the desire to serve his country, and to deliver the oppressed. He sacrificed his own ambition to the great cause of Liberty and Honour, to which he believed he was called by God Himself. His horror of it all made no difference to the doing of what he felt was his duty, even to the laying down of a life which had always been pleasant to him and held so much promise for the future.' He was only twenty-nine when he died, and had he written nothing but those two last poems, which he wrote on active service, would have been sure of his place in our remembrance among the soldier poets of this war.

VII

> The clamorous guns by day and night
>   Toss echoes to and fro,
> White-winged above the dusty fight
>   The ranging war-hawks go,
> And stout King Richard's proud array
>   Is but a shining tale,
> But English courage goes as gay
>   In khaki as in mail.
>
> LIEUT. A. L. JENKINS, *Crusaders*.

I AM not attempting anything of criticism here; I am attempting nothing more than to show in their own words what was in their hearts and minds when these men of peace, these civilians in grain, made soldiers of themselves under stress of necessity, and what was the real object of their fighting. Going about their everyday business in the trenches or in the hurly-burly of conflict, they were like the rest of that incomparable fellowship of our fighting men who, as Lieutenant Coningsby Dawson has it in his *Khaki Courage*, 'wear their crown of thorns as if it were a cap and bells'; but behind the scenes, waiting for their cues to go on again, they opened their inmost thoughts in these verses of theirs, laid bare their ideals and the secret sources of their strength. Without some compelling cause which they could defend with clean consciences, some appeal to what was highest and most chivalrous in them, it is obvious in all they have written that they were not men who could have brought themselves to turn aside from the arts of peace to master the black art of war.

There are lyrics in St. Vincent Morris's little book that are thoughtful, fanciful, steeped in religious earnestness, and more carefully finished than his sonnet, 'The Eleventh Hour,' but there is nothing more simply earnest or more self-revealing. He was the son of Canon Morris, of Ashbourne, Derbyshire. When the war came he was only eighteen, too young for the Army, and the feeling that fretted him while he waited and made him glad to take up his duty as soon as he was old enough, finds an outlet in that sonnet :

> Is this to live ?—to cower and stand aside
>   While others fight and perish day by day ?
>   To see my loved ones slaughtered, and to say :
> ' Bravo ! bravo ! how nobly you have died ! '
> Is this to love ?—to heed my friends no more,
>   But watch them perish in a foreign land
>   Unheeded, and to give no helping hand,
> But smile, and say, ' How terrible is war ! '
>
> Nay, this is not to love, nor this to live !
>   I will go forth ; I hold no more aloof ;
> And I will give all that I have to give,
>   And leave the refuge of my father's roof.
> Then, if I live, no man shall say, think I,
> ' He lives, because he did not dare to die ! '

He left Brighton College in the summer of 1915 and, on 7th August, was gazetted to the 3rd Battalion of the Sherwood Foresters. 'Finding that his chance of getting across to France seemed remote,' says the memoir in his book, ' he transferred in the year following to the Royal Flying Corps. In the spring of 1917 he crossed to France. On 10th April his machine was brought down by a blizzard at Vimy Ridge. His right leg and left thigh were fractured, and he sustained several cuts about the head.' On 29th April he died of his wounds.

A yet more irresistible call to action than Morris's chivalrous love of comrades, was the martyrdom of Belgium. Flight Sub-Lieutenant Frank Lewis was a boy of nineteen when he was killed in France in an air battle. The call that drew him out to France is in the second of two sonnets on ' Belgium, 1914 ' that he wrote in the first months of the war, while he was still at Marlborough :

There came a voice from out the darkness crying—
   A pleading voice, the voice of one in thrall :
Come, ye who pass—oh, heed you not my sighing ?
   Come and deliver ! Hear, oh, hear my call !

For when the invader stood before my gate
   Demanding passage through with haughty tone,
A voice cried loud, ' Wilt thou endure this fate ?
   Better have death than live when honour 's flown ! '
And so my children now lie slain by him
   I had not wronged ; with strife my land is riven ;
Dishonoured here I lie with fettered limb,
   To desecration all my shrines are given,
And nought remains but bondage drear and grim—
   God ! Is there any justice under heaven ? '

This was the cry, too, that Reginald Freston heard and could not but answer :

Suppose, as some have done, I had made excuse,
I, who am poor,
Suppose I had sought seclusion in the dim far lands
    of exile,
Over the leagues of foam ;
And there in warmth and safety, far from the din
    and roar,
Had built me another home !
Surely, had I done this, in the dark still hours of night,
I should have woke from sleep, with my soul in
    great affright,
Hearing the cry of innocent blood
   From over the Eastern wave,
Voices of little children
   That I could but would not save.

But beyond and above even pity for the foully slaughtered children and women of Belgium rose the stronger, holier call to save the sanctuaries of civilisation from the destroyer, and so shatter his power for destruction that the peace of the world and the rights of the weak should never go in fear of it again—a call that rings like a tocsin in some of the noblest poetry of the war.

Though the delightfully frivolous and satirical things in the *Poems and Parodies* of Professor Kettle justify the prefatory description of him as 'a genial cynic,' what the preface says further of his personal charm and his love of humanity are as amply justified in the dedicatory sonnet to his wife—

Faith lasts ? Nay, since I knew your yielded eyes,
I am content with sight . . . of paradise—

in the impassioned appeal 'To Young Ireland'; in the subdued pathos of the lines 'On Leaving Ireland; July 14, 1916,' when in the glow of the sunset he could think only of bayonet flash and bugle call,

 And knew that even I shall fall on sleep.

He notes at the head of these lines that 'the pathos of departure is indubitable,' and adds a reference to his essay 'On Saying Good-Bye.' If you turn to that essay in *The Day's Burden* these are its closing words : ' " However amusing the comedy may have been," wrote Pascal, " there is always blood in the fifth act. They scatter a little dust on your face; and then all is over for ever." Blood there may be, but blood does not necessarily mean tragedy. The wisdom of humility bids us pray that in that fifth act we may have good lines and a timely exit.' Well, he had a brave ending to his fifth act and fell in action, and for the good lines, there could have been none better than his own 'To My Daughter Betty,' written 'on the field, before Guillemont, Somme, September 4, 1916,' telling her that when she grows up she may ask why he abandoned her to dice with death—

> And oh! they'll give you rhyme
> And reason: some will call the thing sublime,
> And some decry it in a knowing tone.
> So here, while the mad guns curse overhead,
> And tired men sigh with mud for couch and floor,
> Know that we fools, now with the foolish dead,
> Died not for flag, nor King, nor Emperor,
> But for a dream, born in a herdsman's shed,
> And for the secret Scriptures of the poor.

That was the great cause he had at heart, and he acclaims it again in his 'Song of the Irish Armies,' which in reality is the song of all our armies, old and new. Sing the old soldiers:

> . . . Not for this did our fathers fall,
> That truth and pity and love and all
> Should break in dust at a trumpet call,
> Yea, all things clean and old.

T. M. Kettle

> Not to this had we sacrificed :
> To sit at the last where the players diced
> With blood-hot hands for the robes of Christ,
> And snatch at the Devil's gold.

Sing the new soldiers :

> To Odin's challenge we cried Amen !
> We stayed the plough and laid by the pen,
> And we shouldered our guns like gentlemen,
> That the wiser weak should hold. . . .

> Time for the plough when the sword has won ;
> The loom will wait on the crashing gun,
> And the hands of Peace drop benison
> When the task of death is through.

Sing the old and new soldiers in unison :

> Then lift the flag of the last Crusade !
> And fill the ranks of the last Brigade !
> March on to the fields where the world's remade,
> And the Ancient Dreams come true !

A typical new marching song, to stand by that, is the powerful protest and appeal, 'Before the Assault,' into which R. E. Vernede has distilled the innermost soul and purpose of the Allied Armies :

If through this roar o' guns one prayer may reach
  Thee,
  Lord of all Life, whose mercies never sleep,
Not in our time, not now, Lord, we beseech Thee
  To grant us peace.   The sword has bit too deep.

We may not rest.   We hear the wail of mothers
  Mourning the sons who fill some nameless grave :
Past us, in dreams, the ghosts march of our brothers
  Who were most valiant . . . whom we could not
    save. . . .

We see all fair things fouled—homes Love's hands
    builded
  Shattered to dust beside their withered vines,
Shattered the towers that once Thy sunsets gilded,
  And Christ struck yet again within His shrines. . . .

We have failed—we have been more weak than
    these betrayers—
  In strength or in faith we have failed ; our pride
    was vain.
How can we rest who have not slain the slayers ?
  What peace for us who have seen Thy children
    slain ?

Hark, the roar grows . . . the thunders reawaken—
  We ask one thing, Lord, only one thing now :
Hearts high as theirs who went to death unshaken,
  Courage like theirs to make and keep their vow :

R. E. Vernede

To stay not till those hosts whom mercies harden,
   Who know no glory save of sword and fire,
Find in our fire the splendour of Thy pardon,
   Meet from our steel the mercy they desire. . . .

Then to our children there shall be no handing
   Of fates so vain—of passions so abhorred. . . .
But Peace . . . the Peace which passeth understanding. . .
   Not in our time . . . but in their time, O Lord.

Vernede had made a name as a writer of fiction and was in his fortieth year when the war burst upon us. He had been educated at St. Paul's School, and at Oxford; and four years after leaving Oxford was, in 1902, married to Miss Carol Howard Fry, and was settled in Hertfordshire, happy in his work and the growth of his literary reputation, when the fatal August 1914 changed everything. Within a month, though he was well beyond military age, he enlisted in the Public Schools Battalion of the 19th Royal Fusiliers as a private. 'He was,' says Mr.

Edmund Gosse, in an introduction to Vernede's *War Poems*, ' without any predilection for military matters and without any leaning to what are called " Jingo " views. But when once the problem of the attack of Germany on the democracy of the world was patent to him, he did not hesitate for a moment.' His profound conviction of the rightness of the cause for which he was to lay down his life runs like a glowing thread through much of his poetry. The selfless aspiration he voices in ' A Petition ' is

That now when envious foes would spoil thy splendour,
   Unversed in arms, a dreamer such as I
May in thy ranks be deemed not all unworthy,
   England, for thee to die.

And he is as fearless and high-hearted in the touching lines ' To C. H. V.' :

What shall I bring to you, wife of mine,
   When I come back from the war ? . . .

R. E. Vernede

Little you 'd care what I laid at your feet,
    Ribbon or crest or shawl—
What if I bring you nothing, Sweet,
    Nor maybe come back at all ?
Ah, but you 'll know, Brave Heart, you 'll know
    Two things I 'll have kept to send :
Mine honour, for which you bade me go,
    And my love—my love to the end.

He went to France as a lieutenant of the 3rd Rifle Brigade ; was wounded in September 1916, was invalided home for a while, but had returned to the front by the end of the year. Scattered through the *Letters to his Wife* are his views on the war, his unbounded admiration of the cheerfulness and courage of his men, his deep resentment of the crimes of Germany and his conviction that there could be no safety for the world and no peace till the Allies had fought on to victory. Here from various letters are some of the things he wrote : ' I still think it right that war should be damnable, but I wish everybody could have an idea of how beastly it can be. . . . The papers are so complaisant over every little success that they are almost bound to be equally downhearted over every failure—don't believe them. Only believe that we shall win in the end. . . . The Germans seem to have been behaving abominably; that is in keeping with their traditions apparently, but it makes me feel that they won't realise the war till they have had their own houses deliberately blown up by a number of insulting fiends. Losing colonies or navies doesn't affect the individuals at all closely, and though they mayn't have the guilt of their government, I think they have to bear the punishment of the crimes they commit to order.' He hopes that when the war is past ' people won't altogether forget it in our generation. That's what I wanted to say in the verses I began about—

> Not in our time, O Lord, we now beseech Thee
> To grant us peace—the sword has bit too deep—

but never got on with. What I mean is that for us there can be no real forgetting. We have seen too much of it, known too many people's sorrow, felt it too much, to return to an existence in which it has no part.' He finishes a letter dated 8th April 1917: 'I think it will be summer soon, and perhaps the war will end this year and I shall see my Pretty One again.' Next day he fell mortally wounded, leading an attack on Havricourt Wood.

In easier times we have sorrowed over the untimely fate of the young poet who has died with all his promise unfulfilled. Here is not merely one such, but a great and goodly company of poets, and in face of a tragedy so immeasurable, a loss so utterly beyond reckoning, words become idle and meaningless. It is something, it is much, to all those whose sons, husbands, brothers, lovers they were that their country shall hold them for ever in grateful remembrance, something that these songs of theirs shall live and their names be written imperishably in the records of these terrible years; but the greater consolation has been written by themselves—by Lieutenant Cyril Winterbotham, in ' The Cross of Wood ' :

God be with you and us who go our way
And leave you dead upon the ground you won;
For you at last the long fatigue is done,
The hard march ended; you have rest to-day.

You were our friends, with you we watched the dawn
Gleam through the rain of the long winter night,
With you we laboured till the morning light
Broke on the village, shell-destroyed and torn.

Not now for you the glorious return
To steep Stroud valleys, to the Severn leas
By Tewkesbury and Gloucester, or the trees
Of Cheltenham under high Cotswold stern.

For you no medals such as others wear—
A cross of bronze for those approvèd brave—
To you is given, above a shallow grave,
The Wooden Cross that marks your resting there.

> Rest you content, more honourable far
> Than all the Orders is the Cross of Wood,
> The symbol of self-sacrifice that stood
> Bearing the God whose brethren you are.

—and by Lieutenant St. Vincent Morris in the poem to a friend, whose home the war has left desolate, bidding her be comforted:

> Still do you grieve, in that your loved one lies
>   Beneath some lonely, unforgotten grave. . . .
> Like an immortal offering sacrificed?
> Because he died that others might not die?
>
>   And yet, and yet,
> Even though sorrow Love may not forget,
>   Such was the death of Christ.
>
> Comfort, sad heart! Beyond that little grave
>   Rests an immortal soul in God's repose:
> 'Others He saved, Himself He could not save,'
>   This was the task he chose.
> Your love is crucified on that small cross,
> That lonely Sentinel where he has trod,
> Leaving thereon all trace of grief and loss.
>
>   And then your love
> Will rise to find him where he waits above
>   Before the throne of God.

VIII

> But God grant your dear England
>   A strength that shall not cease
> Till she have won for all the earth
>   From ruthless men release,
> And made supreme upon her
> Mercy and Truth and Honour——
> Is this the thing you died for?
>   O brothers, sleep in peace.
>
>   LIEUT. R. E. VERNEDE, *To Our Fallen.*

IF one may say so without seeming boastful I sometimes wonder whether, just now, there are not too many apologists among us—too many well-meaning persons who paint our national past in darker colours than belong to it and write as if the war had lifted us to heights we had not trodden before? War cannot endow a nation with qualities it does not already possess; it is merely the acid which tests the metal and proves it to be either gold or a base imitation. At the risk of repeating myself, I want to emphasise that the minds and souls of the forty-four soldier poets whose work we have been considering—and they and their many living peers have spoken for the general mind and soul of our people—were not formed on the battlefield; their opinions, ideals, aspirations were engendered in the home atmosphere during years of peace. We and our Allies, and Germany and her Allies remain in this war what racial instincts, long traditions, and peace-time training had naturally made of us all. The war did not make us or them one thing or the other; it did no more than give those who went into it opportunity to show whether they were beast or human, and I, for one, am not ashamed of the witness it has borne to the inherent character of my countrymen.

German professors, inflated with envy and a ridiculous pride in that German culture which has culminated in poison-gas, piracy, and the murder of civilians, have denounced us as land-grabbers and bloodthirsty; and no answer to that charge seems necessary beyond a comparison of the widely different ways in which the British and German empires have been built. Fifty years ago Prussia resolved to transform itself into a great empire. To this end, it picked a quarrel with its neighbour Austria and defeated her. Then it attacked its small neighbour Denmark, broke her, and stole one of her provinces. Then it brought about a war with France, crushed her and stole two provinces from her. Then, having menaced or persuaded the weaker German states into combining with it, it settled down to forty years of subtle, strenuous preparation on a gigantic scale with the avowed object of seizing Belgium, and more of France, and annexing divers other lands by murderous, irresistible might and so achieving a mammoth empire and world domination. The fruit of its labour is an

For Remembrance

empire that has sprung up like the unwholesome fungus-growth of a night, and the signs are that it will be as transitory as any toadstool.

Never at any period of her history has Britain developed in this furtive and obscene fashion. Our empire is not the realisation of any deliberate plan; it has come into being gradually and by accident rather than by design; it has grown slowly and healthfully through the centuries as an oak grows, and its strength and its justification are in that. Our sons took their lives in their hands and went exploring on their own account into savage regions and settled down and colonised the waste places of the earth; our merchant adventurers sailed into unknown parts to do business among strange races and establish markets where none had been before. They had little enough encouragement and often the most crass discouragement from their own government, which was so far from dreaming of conquest that not infrequently it extended its protection to its wandering children with reluctance and formally took over the control of this or that uncivilised land not to colonise it, but because its subjects had colonised it already. Germany's wise professors even sneered at our inefficiency as empire-builders, because we had gone about it so unscientifically and did not really govern our colonies; we had not efficiently riveted them to us as with iron bands; we did not rule them, but left them to rule themselves. If ever we were in danger they would not take the risk of coming to our assistance, and, inept, incompetent rulers as we are, we could not compel them to do so—they would gladly seize upon our necessity as a chance to cut themselves free of us altogether and leave us to our fate. So said the German professors, and the war has revealed the measure of their knowledge. No sooner were we

Photo by Elliott & Fry.

R. E. VERNÈDE.
LIEUT., RIFLE BRIGADE.

threatened than our kindred overseas were by our side, ready to stand or to fall with us.

Not because of our perfections. We know that, and they know it. We have made mistakes, we have done many wrongs, we have been foolish and faulty in our time, as fallible human creatures were bound to be. Our own sons in the homeland, ' who,' as Noel Hodgson says of his fallen comrades :

> Who loving as none other
> The land that is their mother,
> Unfalteringly renounced her
> Because they loved her so—

did no more, maybe, than the sons of any land might do, but they did it with an eagerness and a joy in the self-sacrifice that could not have been possible to them had they been dying for a land that was all unworthy of them. Nor was it solely because they were more or less distantly of our blood that Canada, Australasia,

South Africa, and the rest of our scattered commonwealth remained so loyal to us. It touches us with pride and yet humbles us to think we can glimpse something of Canada's thought and feeling towards ' Britain ' in these glowing lines by one of Canada's poets, Wilfred Campbell, who has died since the war moved his nation to prove that his were no empty words :

Great patient Titan, 'neath thy wearying load
    Of modern statecraft, human helpfulness ;
    To whom do come earth's weak in their distress
To crave thine arm to avert the oppressor's goad :
Thou sovereignty within thine isled abode,
    Hated and feared, where thou wouldst only bless,
    By fools who dream thine iron mightiness
Will crumble in ruin across the world's wide road.

Though scattered thy sons o'er leagues of empire's rim,
    Alien, remote, by severing wind and tide ;
Yet every Briton who knows thy blood in him
    In that dread hour will marshal to thy side ;
And if thou crumblest earth's whole frame will groan.
God help this world, thou wilt not sink alone !

The innermost secret of that faith in Britain and that spontaneous loyalty to her—the real reason why our kindred, who are separated from us and have shaped themselves into new, independent nations, feel that Britain is still worth fighting and dying for is enshrined again, I think, in a poem by an Australian, John Farrel, who has been dead these fourteen years. He and his countrymen know the worst of us, but they know the best of us too, and believe that the best more than atones for the worst. No enemy has indicted us more scathingly than he, in his 'Australia to England.' He does not forget that we have lapsed into evil, have been guilty of sins of greed, cruelty, hypocrisy; that

> Some hands you taught to pray to Christ
> Have prayed His curse to rest on you—

yet, when he has reckoned up all our grievous errors, he can find it in his heart to add:

But praise to you and more than praise
   And thankfulness for some things done,
And blessedness and length of days
   As long as earth shall last, or sun !
You first among the peoples spoke
   Sharp words and angry questionings
Which burst the bonds and shed the yoke
   That made your men the slaves of kings !

You set and showed the whole world's school
   The lesson it shall surely read,
That each one ruled has right to rule—
   The alphabet of Freedom's creed,
Which slowly wins its proselytes
   And makes uneasy many a throne :
You taught them all to prate of Rights
   In language growing like your own.

And now your holiest and best
   And wisest dream of such a tie
As, holding hearts from East to West,
   Shall strengthen while the years go by ;
And of a time when every man
   For every fellow-man will do
His kindliest, working by the plan
   God set him. May the dream come true !

> And greater dreams ! O Englishmen,
>   Be sure the safest time of all
> For even the mightiest State is when
>   Not even the least desires its fall !
> Make England stand supreme for aye
>   Because supreme for peace and good,
> Warned well by wrecks of yesterday
>   That strongest feet may slip in blood !

Here, then, is why the men of the free nations of Greater Britain have cast in their lot with ours to-day — because though we have stumbled too often and lost the way, we have still struggled back into it and moved, however haltingly, through all our divagations, towards a final goal of freedom and universal brotherhood, towards the ideal of a world ruled by love and not by terror. Neither now nor at any period have we made war our national industry; we have never at any period hammered our whole people into one vast army for the subjugation and enslavement of our neighbours. Whatever sin we have committed, we have never committed that sin. Our literature for centuries past testifies that though, the world being what it is, we have put our causes to the arbitrament of the sword, we have hated war, and the wrong and misery of it, with a steadily increasing hatred.

Among the stirring and splendidly patriotic thunderings of *Henry V.*, Shakespeare puts into the mouths of the unlettered soldiery of his day a most poignant sense of the heavy responsibility their ruler will bear if he sends them to kill and be killed in a fight that is not just. Addison's verses on the battle of Blenheim give an elegant and flattering picture of Marlborough in the hour of triumph, but you need not grudge the Duke his compliment, for, when in due season he died, Swift wrote the satirical elegy upon him that is surely the bitterest, most mordant protest ever raised against a successful war and its commander:

> Behold his funeral appears:
> No widows' sighs nor orphans' tears,
> Wont at such times each heart to pierce,
> Attend the progress of his hearse.
> But what of that? his friends may say—
> He had those honours in his day:
> True to his profit and his pride,
> He made them weep before he died.

And in the next century, Southey took the same theme and, in his gentler vein, satirised the Duke and his triumph in 'The Battle of Blenheim,' where old Kaspar, moralising over the skull found on the battlefield, is unable to explain why the victory was a great and a famous one and can only reiterate, to the end, that it was that:

> ' But what good came of it at last?'
>   Quoth little Peterkin.
> ' Why, that I cannot tell,' said he,
> ' But 'twas a famous victory.'

Since then, we have come more and more, as a nation, to little Peterkin's outlook on this matter of war. We are more insistently asking why it should survive among rational Christian people, what is the good of it, with its brutalities, its waste, its suffering and heartbreak, and all the harm it does? And we grow less and less contented with the mechanical explanation of non-combatant philosophers and professors that it is a biological necessity, a natural, recurring phase in our social evolution, and its miseries the inevitable price of human progress, that it is a glorious institution and serves to preserve the breed of heroes as racing preserves that of horses. We know, or if any do not they may know it from what has been written by our soldiers themselves, that there is no glory and little romance in war except for those who can play with the thought of it from far off, or after the years have healed its wounds and hidden the hideous ruin it wrought, and the agony of it has dwindled to the glamorous sorrow of a tale that is told.

Byron on the field of Waterloo felt no exultant thrill: to him it was a 'place of skulls,' where 'the red rain hath made the harvest grow,' and it reminded him only of the

> Vain years
> Of death, depopulation, bondage, tears

which had gone to the making of that Emperor's pride who, as utterly shorn of it all as if he had never possessed any, was then eating his heart out at St. Helena. The withering contempt for the pompous vanity of the military conqueror in Byron's 'Ode to Napoleon,' and his admiration of America's clean-handed patriot-ruler are things we should do well also to remember now, when Europe is cursed with a pettier tyrant who has assumed the part of the dead lion and cannot roar without betraying himself :

> Where may the wearied eye repose,
>   When gazing on the Great,
> Where neither guilty glory glows
>   Nor despicable state ?
> Yet one—the first—the last—the best—
> The Cincinnatus of the West,
>   Whom envy dared not hate,
> Bequeathed the name of Washington,
> To make man blush there was but one.

Time has taken the sting out of that last line : there has been Lincoln ; there is Wilson ; to say nothing of others ; and it seems likely that in the future Wilson's name will, like Abou Ben Adhem's, ' lead all the rest.'

America has come into this war with such ideals as took us into it, and her attitude towards all war is the same as our own. She has no use for its pinchbeck glory, but looks beyond all that and sees what Longfellow saw when he wrote ' Killed at the Ford ' :

> I saw in a vision how, far and fleet,
> That fatal bullet went speeding forth
> Till it reached a town in the distant North,
> Till it reached a house in a sunny street,
> Till it reached a heart that ceased to beat
> Without a murmur, without a cry.

For the blood-drops on the conqueror's laurel are not from the brow that wears it. During that war of North and South which stirred the conscience of America to its depths the Quaker Whittier sorrowed in his poems *In War Time* that a democratic people should have no other but the old world's barbarous way of settling its differences, saying, as we are saying at present:

>   The future's gain
> Is certain as God's truth; but meanwhile, pain
> Is bitter and tears are salt; our voices take
> A sober tone; our very household songs
> Are heavy with a nation's griefs and wrongs;
> And innocent mirth is chastened for the sake
> Of the brave hearts that never more shall beat,
> The eyes that smile no more, the unreturning feet.

It was one of Washington's countrymen, too, James Russell Lowell, who raised the great rallying cry of all civilised democracies, insisted on the soldier's personal responsibility for the right or wrong that he does, and, in *The Biglow Papers*, spoke the nakedest truths that have ever been spoken about war and its makers:

> Ez for war, I call it murder—
>   There you hev it plain and flat;
> I don't want to go no furder
>   Than my Testament fer that. . . .
>
> Ef you take a sword and dror it
>   An' go stick a feller thru,
> Gov'ment ain't to answer for it,
>   God 'll send the bill to you.

That is the essentially modern standard, and nothing but the obsolete ideas that persist in backward nationalities prevents the civilised world from living up to it. You get no conception except of the pity and barbarism of war in the realistic scenes and ironic comment of Thomas

Hardy's great epic-drama, *The Dynasts*, or in the sombre *War Poems* he wrote during the struggle of Briton and Boer. He is oppressed with the needless tragedy of it all—that ' this late age of thought ' can only argue in the old bloody mode, and marvels—

> When shall the saner, softer polities,
> Whereof we dream, have play in each proud land,
> And patriotism, grown Godlike, scorn to stand
> Bondslave to realms, but circle earth and seas ?

a question to which thinking men of all nations that have outgrown the crudities of their childhood are striving now to find an answer. The one hope that beacons us through these dark days is that the shameful savageries of the Great War, its indescribable horrors, its devastating insanities may shock mankind into so much of practical wisdom that the peoples of every race and creed shall, in self-defence, draw together at last into some league of free nations, some bond of common fellowship that shall end the reign of the brute for ever and realise Tennyson's prevision of a time when disputes between men were no longer settled as they are between animals, but

> The battle-flags were furled
> In the Parliament of Man, the Federation of the world.

THE END

www.ingramcontent.com/pod-product-compliance
Lightning Source LLC
Chambersburg PA
CBHW032102090426
42743CB00007B/205